MANAGING EXCHANGE RATES

D1028144

MANAGING EXCHANGE RATES

Peter B. Kenen

PUBLISHED IN NORTH AMERICA FOR
THE ROYAL INSTITUTE OF INTERNATIONAL AFFAIRS

COUNCIL ON FOREIGN RELATIONS PRESS
NEW YORK

Chatham House Papers

General Series Editor: William Wallace
International Economics Programme Director: DeAnne Julius

The Royal Institute of International Affairs, at Chatham House in London, has provided an impartial forum for discussion and debate on current international issues for 70 years. Its resident research fellows, specialized information resources, and range of publications, conferences, and meetings span the fields of international politics, economics, and security. The Institute is independent of government.

Chatham House Papers are short monographs on current policy problems which have been commissioned by the RIIA. In preparing the papers, authors are advised by a study group of experts convened by the RIIA, and publication of a paper indicates that the Institute regards it as an authoritative contribution to the public debate. The Institute does not, however, hold opinions of its own; the views expressed in this publication are the responsibility of the author.

Library of Congress Cataloguing-in-Publication Data

Kenen, Peter B., 1932–
    Managing exchange rates / by Peter B. Kenen.
        p.   cm. — (Chatham House papers)
    British ed. published: London : Royal Institute of International Affairs : London : New York : Routledge, 1988.
    Bibliography: p.
    ISBN 0-87609-061-7 : $14.95
    1. Foreign exchange administration. I. Title.   II. Series: Chatham House papers (Unnumbered)
[HG3851.K365   1989]
332.4'56–dc20
                                                        89–32091
                                                        CIP

88 89 90 91 92 93 94 95 PB 10 9 8 7 6 5 4 3 2 1

CONTENTS

ACKNOWLEDGMENTS

This paper was written during my sabbatical leave from Princeton University, financed partly by the Royal Institute of International Affairs and partly by a fellowship from the German Marshall Fund of the United States. I am deeply grateful to Chatham House, not only for financial support but also for providing a challenging and cordial environment and for organizing the study group which gave me much helpful advice and criticism. Special thanks go to Dr DeAnne Julius and her colleagues in the International Economics Programme.

July 1988   Peter B. Kenen

The International Economics Programme

The project which gave rise to this paper forms part of the International Economics Programme of the Royal Institute of International Affairs. This programme seeks to provide clear analyses and practical policy recommendations for resolving international economic conflicts and strengthening the functioning of the world economy. It covers the economics and international politics of monetary, trade, finance, and investment issues.

Sponsors of the Programme include American Express Bank, Bank of England, The BOC Group, Department of Trade and Industry, HM Treasury, Lloyds Bank, Merrill Lynch, Midland Bank, Morgan Grenfell, Royal International, RTZ, and S.G. Warburg.

1

INTRODUCTION

Ideas lead lives of their own, and some are almost immortal. They may have little influence for long periods, but events can revive them abruptly. When that happens, however, they wear old-fashioned clothing and speak in quaint phrases. They need to be brought up to date. This monograph tries to perform that task for an idea that has been revived rather suddenly – the idea that governments should manage exchange rates.

For twenty-five years following World War II, exchange-rate arrangements were governed by the Bretton Woods System. The rules of the system were laid down in the Articles of Agreement of the International Monetary Fund (IMF). Its actual functioning reflected the dominant role of the United States in the world economy and the even more dominant role of the US dollar. Under the Bretton Woods System, exchange rates were pegged. They could be changed occasionally, devalued or revalued, to compensate for fundamental changes in the economic situation. For the most part, however, they were confined to very narrow bands. Governments intervened on foreign-exchange markets to keep rates within those bands, while taking other measures, including monetary and fiscal measures, to remove or reduce the market pressures that threatened to drive rates beyond their bands.

At the end of the 1960s, the United States faced an intractable conflict between its domestic economic objectives and its international obligations. Its attempt to resolve the conflict by changing its exchange rate led to the breakdown of the Bretton Woods System.

Introduction

Early in 1973, the major industrial countries moved from pegged to floating exchange rates.

At first, the switch was expected to be temporary. A Committee on Reform of the International Monetary System, commonly called the Committee of Twenty, was appointed to produce a new pegged-rate system more flexible and symmetrical than the Bretton Woods System – one that would give the United States more freedom to change it own exchange rate but less freedom to exploit what Charles de Gaulle had called the 'exorbitant privilege' of the dollar.

In the interim, however, governments had persuaded themselves that floating was better than pegging, and that it was impossible in any case to return to pegged exchange rates under conditions prevailing in the mid-1970s. They were encouraged in this view by the majority of academic economists, who had come to favour floating rates long before the switch in 1973. And the next generation of officials, believing that markets are wiser than governments, was even more comfortable with floating rates. They were prepared to blame their own policies, or those of other governments, when exchange rates moved in ways that were not to their liking.

Governments did not refrain completely from trying to influence exchange rates. They voiced views about 'appropriate' rates to influence the markets' views, and they intervened from time to time to resist exchange-rate changes. In 1977, for example, Michael Blumenthal, US Secretary of the Treasury, said that he would welcome an appreciation of certain other currencies against the dollar, and the dollar began to depreciate. In 1978, after the dollar had fallen sharply for more than a year, it was stabilized briefly by large-scale intervention. In 1979, moreover, members of the European Community established the European Monetary System (EMS) to peg exchange rates connecting their own currencies and provide extensive credit facilities for financing the intervention needed to defend those rates.

No attempt was made, however, to stabilize the key exchange rates connecting the dollar, yen, and mark, and governments declared repeatedly that they should not do so. It would be wrong in principle for them to second-guess the markets' views and futile in practice to pit their own resources against the vast amounts of private capital that might be bet against them. They watched with remarkable detachment the appreciation of the dollar that began in 1980 and went on for four more years, raising its average value by more than 50 per cent in terms of other currencies. Many US officials actually took pride in the appreciation, despite the domestic dislocation it was causing and the huge trade deficit to which it was contributing. They said that markets were showing their confidence in the policies of the Reagan administration.

But a new view began to emerge in 1985, and a new activism followed. In September 1985, the five key-currency countries (France, West Germany, Japan, the United Kingdom, and the United States), known as the G-5, chided foreign-exchange markets for failing to take full account of changes in national policies and other 'fundamentals' affecting exchange rates. They called on markets to bring the dollar down and thus bring it into line with the fundamentals, and warned that they would intervene when and if that would be helpful.

That declaration, the Plaza Communiqué, was followed in February 1987 by the Louvre Accord, in which the governments went further. In 1985, they had agreed on the 'wrongness' of current exchange rates, which was not difficult in light of the large US trade deficit and resulting protectionist pressures. In 1987, they agreed on the 'rightness' of current exchange rates – that the dollar had fallen far enough – and said that they would stabilize them temporarily.*

Exchange rates were fairly stable in the months that followed, thanks largely to official intervention, and some officials began to contemplate more formal, long-lasting arrangements. They fell silent in October, however, when the dollar weakened again in the wake of the stock-market crash, and they have been more cautious since. This more cautious mood was not a mere swing of the pendulum, a reaction to the disappointments of 1987. Officials began to remember the questions that plagued them years ago – questions much harder than those they must confront when taking *ad hoc* measures to drive the dollar down or stabilize it temporarily.

It is not hard to promise that exchange rates will be stabilized until further notice. It is far harder to decide when to give that notice – how and when to realign the structure of exchange rates. It is not hard to plan a single act of intervention aimed at changing expec-

---

*The Louvre Accord was to have been issued by the G-5 plus Canada and Italy, known as the G-7, but Italy objected to endorsing a draft prepared in advance by the G-5. Subsequent statements, however, have been issued by the G-7, and that term is used hereafter to identify the group of governments that are most heavily involved in exchange-rate management and policy coordination.

3

tations in the foreign-exchange market. It is far harder to design long-lasting rules for exchange-rate management, which necessarily translate into rules and arrangements for creating and holding reserves and have far-reaching implications for monetary policies. These challenges raise the problems of symmetry and leadership that cropped up years ago in the Committee of Twenty. They turn quickly and concretely into questions and concerns about US policies and the US dollar.

This monograph deals with some of those questions, brought up to date by recent research and experience. It looks with particular care at the workings and achievements of the EMS and at efforts to manage exchange rates under the Plaza and Louvre agreements.

Answers to some of those questions will be shown to depend on the way that we interpret controversial evidence about the functioning of foreign-exchange markets. There is disagreement, for example, about the manner in which markets form their expectations, a matter decisive for judging the governments' ability to influence those expectations by changing or promising to change their policies. There is disagreement about the extent of substitutability among assets denominated in different currencies, a matter decisive for judging the effectiveness of official intervention and the need for coordinating monetary policies to foster exchange-rate stability. Answers to other important questions will be shown to depend on highly subjective judgments about policy-making processes in the United States and other countries – whether there is hope of making them more flexible and less parochial.

I will not conceal my personal views about these matters, even those that are mainly political. They are crucial to my main conclusion. Exchange rates should be managed, not left completely to market forces, but informal arrangements such as those exemplified by the Plaza and Louvre agreements may not suffice. To manage exchange rates effectively over the long term, it may be necessary to manage them systematically, not episodically, and thus to devise a pegged-rate system resembling the EMS.

Those who have studied the EMS closely point to special circumstances that have helped it to function effectively: its intimate connection with the European Community, the deep concern with inflation that attracted European governments to the discipline of a pegged-rate system, and the central role of Germany, a role similar in prominence but different in substance from the role of the United

States in the Bretton Woods System. These special circumstances necessarily limit the applicability of lessons learned from the EMS experience. They also warn of the need to confront the concern expressed frequently in Europe, that the United States cannot be trusted to discharge the obligations of economic leadership that would be thrust upon it by a more tightly managed system.

This monograph has five more chapters. Chapter 2 reviews in some detail the monetary history summarized above and explores the rationale for managing exchange rates. Chapter 3 looks at ways of managing exchange rates, including the methods actually used during the last forty years and some of those proposed but not yet tested.

Chapter 4 is addressed to the central question: Can exchange rates be managed by informal, confidential understandings among governments, or is it necessary to adopt more formal arrangements? The case for formal arrangements, based on firm and transparent commitments, derives from the need for governments to maintain credibility in their dealings with the foreign-exchange market. Formal commitments are risky, because credibility is gravely damaged when governments back away from them. But imprecise commitments are risky too, because governments and markets can misinterpret them, with results that undermine the markets' confidence in the governments' commitments.

Chapters 5 and 6 examine the much larger issues that crop up when we start to contemplate a tightly managed system. What should be the roles of intervention and reserves in exchange-rate management? Are there ways to reduce the dependence of the monetary system on the US dollar? How closely must governments coordinate their policies under a tightly managed system? Is it necessary to coordinate fiscal policies as well as monetary policies? And Chapter 6 concludes by posing one more question: What are the costs and benefits of a tightly managed system? That is the question on which the issue will be decided.

2
THE RATIONALE FOR MANAGING EXCHANGE RATES

Introduction

Prices convey information. At one level, they define the terms on which goods, services, and assets can be traded or, more generally, the terms on which purchasing power – income or wealth – can be used to buy them. At another level, they embody information that households, firms, and governments have used in making decisions. The information is not always up to date, because most prices are revised periodically, not altered continuously. It is not always accurate, because the decisions reflected by prices are based on imperfect information, including best guesses about the future. And it is not always complete, because those who have the greatest influence on markets are motivated by objectives and concerns that focus on particular bits of information, such as average opinion today about average opinion tomorrow.[1]

Economists tend to idealize the information embodied in prices. Much current economic theory is based on the rational expectations hypothesis, which asserts that decision-makers use *all* the available information and process it accurately, and on the equally unrealistic supposition that prices adjust instantaneously and thus reflect information promptly and completely. Even those economists who reject these suppositions retain a great deal of faith in the quality of the information conveyed by prices. If it were not knowledge but mere noise, economics would be empty. Therefore, economists are hostile to schemes and policies that would fix or manage prices.

Nevertheless, a number of economists have begun to say that exchange rates should be managed, even though the exchange rate is the most important single price for any economy. Being the price of one national currency in terms of another, it is the link between *all* prices quoted in that currency and their counterparts in other countries' currencies – not only the prices of goods and services but also those of real and financial assets.

Why should economists favour the management of this crucial price when they deplore the management of most other prices?

Some would answer along lines reflecting my warning about the quality of information conveyed by prices in general. When exchange rates are determined by market forces, they necessarily reflect the sorts of information that market participants deem to be important. This limits their usefulness to those decision-makers who must translate other prices from currency to currency, buyers of goods, services, and assets, and those who are charged with making long-term business decisions – what to produce and where to produce it. On this view, exchange rates are too important to be left to market forces.

Others would answer by invoking a different proposition. Because an exchange rate is the price of one money in terms of another, changes in money supplies are bound to affect exchange rates. Conversely, a commitment to manage exchange rates is an implicit constraint on the management of money, and those who believe that the managers of money must themselves be managed – subjected to some sort of discipline or rule – regard the fixing or pegging of exchange rates as the most effective rule. They readily concede that it may not be sufficient. If the managers of money in every country conspired to behave irresponsibly, they could honour the rule but flout its purpose. Therefore, something more is needed, a limitation on global monetary growth, which is the core of the case for the classical gold standard and for the 'gold standard without gold' proposed by McKinnon (1984). But that additional limitation can function effectively only in tandem with an exchange-rate rule.

Both of these answers embody complicated judgments about economics and politics – about the ways that markets and governments behave – and judgments of this sort are unavoidable. Too often, however, they are badly biased. We tend to compare the actual functioning of the current exchange-rate regime, which is strongly affected by uncertainties and rigidities in the world

7

economy and by imperfect policies, with the hypothetical functioning of some other regime imbedded in a simple theoretical model.

Many made this error twenty years ago, when they came to favour floating rates. They compared the actual behaviour of the Bretton Woods System, based on pegged exchange rates, with an idealized floating-rate system. That particular comparison was very badly flawed, because it relied on theoretical models that made two predictions. First, floating exchange rates would move slowly and smoothly, because their behaviour depended mainly on current-account flows – on purchases of currencies to pay for goods and services – and the basic determinants of those flows tend to change quite gradually. Second, floating rates would reduce economic interdependence, permitting each government to choose its own policies and insulating each economy from other countries' policies. In that framework, then, it was not necessary to assume that governments would follow sensible policies under a floating-rate regime. The attractiveness of floating rates, compared with pegged rates, was actually enhanced by conceding that governments are fallible and apt to pursue parochial objectives.

We know now that those models were pitifully inadequate.[2] The short-run behaviour of a floating exchange rate is not determined by current-account flows. It is determined mainly by capital-account flows, which reflect the highly volatile views of various asset holders. Exchange rates can change hugely from day to day and week to week, and there can be large cumulative movements lasting for three or four years. Exchange rates behave like other asset prices, changing more frequently and rapidly than goods prices and responding to different sorts of information. Therefore, a change in a *nominal* exchange rate, the price of one currency in terms of another, can alter the *real* exchange rate, the prices of one country's goods in terms of other countries' goods. It can thus influence the level, location, and composition of economic activity. For this same reason, moreover, floating exchange rates cannot reduce economic interdependence. They can only alter the *form* of interdependence. Indeed, they produce a peculiarly painful form of interdependence, because monetary and fiscal policies, as well as non-policy shocks, impinge directly on the real economy by affecting the real exchange rate.

Although we have learned a lot about exchange-rate behaviour and economic interdependence under floating exchange rates, we would make another badly biased comparison by failing to recall the lessons we learned earlier about the functioning of pegged exchange rates. We are sadly familiar with the turbulent history of the 1970s and 1980s, when floating rates were buffeted by large shocks and shifts in policies. We tend to idealize the early years of the Bretton Woods System as a golden age of rapid growth and price stability in which balance-of-payments problems were solved easily and inexpensively.[3] According to this highly stylized view, the pegged-rate system functioned well until the United States made two mistakes: getting into the Vietnam war and failing to finance it by raising taxes. We forget the huge swing in commodity prices that surrounded the outbreak of the Korean war, the periodic balance-of-payments crises in Britain and France, even in Japan, and the first round of balance-of-payments problems experienced by the United States in the early 1960s, before the Vietnam war.

We tend also to forget the three complaints made against the workings of the Bretton Woods System. First, the central role of the US dollar made the performance of the world economy heavily dependent on US policies but shielded those policies from external pressures. Second, reliance on the dollar as a reserve asset threatened the stability of the system. Increasing the quantity of dollar reserves would erode the holders' confidence in their quality and undermine the system eventually, but halting the creation of dollar reserves would cause a shortage of reserves and a competitive scramble for them.[4] Third, the exchange-rate regime became too rigid. Governments defended their exchange rates tenaciously, so that changes in rates were too late and too large.

The choice between floating and pegged rates necessarily involves a comparison between the imperfect decision-making powers of markets and governments. Which of them can be expected to manage exchange rates in the more sensible, timely way, holding them stable when changes are not needed but changing them promptly when changes are required? When talking about management by governments, moreover, we must ask another question: How best can governments resolve disagreements concerning the need to change exchange rates?

Highlights in the history of exchange-rate management
The exchange rate is nearly unique among economic variables. It does not belong to any single country but is shared between two

countries. When we know the price of the mark expressed in yen, we know the price of the yen expressed in marks. And this simple bit of arithmetic leads to another. In a world comprising N independent countries, there are only $N - 1$ independent exchange rates. It is therefore impossible for one government to opt for a floating rate if all other governments opt for pegged rates, and it is likewise impossible for all governments to pursue independent exchange-rate targets.[5] International monetary history illustrates the several ways in which this problem can be handled.

Awareness of the problem and of its earlier manifestations heavily influenced the authors of the Bretton Woods Agreement. Failure to confront it in the 1920s had produced an unsustainable pattern of exchange rates:

> An exchange rate by definition concerns more currencies than one. Yet exchange stabilization was carried out as an act of national sovereignty in one country after another with little or no regard to cost and price levels. This was so even where help was received from financial centres abroad. Stabilization of a currency was conceived in terms of gold rather than of other currencies. ...
>
> The two most familiar but by no means the only sources of disequilibrium arose from the successive stabilization of the pound sterling and the French franc early in 1925 and late in 1926 respectively, the one at too high and the other at too low a level in relation to domestic costs and prices. The piecemeal and haphazard manner of international monetary reconstruction sowed the seeds of subsequent disintegration (League of Nations, 1944, pp. 116–17).

Therefore, the authors of the Bretton Woods Agreement sought to introduce collective supervision of exchange-rate policies. Each member of the International Monetary Fund was required to propose a par value for its currency in terms of gold, to obtain IMF approval for that par value, and to keep the exchange rate for its currency within 1 per cent of the parity corresponding to its par value. Thereafter, a government could change its par value only to correct a 'fundamental disequilibrium' and only with the Fund's approval.[6] But the Fund was not allowed to recommend or initiate changes in par values.

Since the value of the US dollar was defined in terms of gold, the fixing of par values in terms of gold automatically implied fixed parities in terms of the dollar. To keep their exchange rates close to those fixed parities, governments bought and sold dollars against their own currencies. The dollar became the main intervention currency, which helped to make it the principal reserve currency. Because these arrangements stabilized the dollar in terms of other currencies, the United States did not have to intervene on foreign-exchange markets. But it was assigned another task under the Bretton Woods Agreement. It was supposed to buy and sell gold, so that other governments acquiring dollars from the foreign-exchange market would not have to hold them but could convert them into gold.

The system was thus symmetrical in principle, although it proved to be less symmetrical in practice. Many governments chose to accumulate dollars instead of buying gold. They did so voluntarily for many years but were obliged to do so later, when US gold holdings were no longer large enough for the United States to honour its side of the bargain. Furthermore, the collective super-vision of exchange-rate policies did not work well. Governments sought approval from the IMF before changing their exchange rates, but they obtained it routinely. In fact, they rarely gave the Fund time to reflect and object. Disagreements about exchange-rate matters were avoided only because the United States had no need to pursue an exchange-rate policy. It functioned as a passive Nth country.

Histories of the international monetary system stress the dominant role of the dollar. That dominance was based at first on the uniquely strong economic position of the United States, reflected in the so-called dollar shortage, which relieved it of concern about its own exchange rate. It could afford to be passive. Its passivity did not imply indifference to the exchange-rate policies of other govern-ments. In 1949, for example, the United States actively urged the devaluation of sterling. But its views reflected its judgments about other governments' exchange-rate policies, not about the implica-tions for the dollar.

The situation began to change in the 1960s, however, when the United States started to run balance-of-payments deficits. Its views about the policies of other governments came to be coloured by its own concerns. In 1961, for example, Germany and the Netherlands

11

revalued their currencies by 5 per cent in response to pressures from Washington. In 1964, the United States opposed a devaluation of the pound, fearing that it would deflect speculative pressures onto the weak dollar; it took the lead in organizing financial support for sterling, and the devaluation was postponed until 1967. Finally, in 1968, Washington sided with France in a dispute with Germany. Paris sought a revaluation of the mark to reduce the French balance-of-payments deficit, but Bonn favoured a devaluation of the franc. Washington backed Paris because a revaluation of the mark would be a partial devaluation of the dollar, which would help the United States with its own balance-of-payments problem, whereas a devaluation of the franc would be a partial revaluation of the dollar, which would exacerbate the US problem.[7]

In 1970, moreover, the US balance of payments deteriorated sharply, and the United States had to adopt an active exchange-rate policy – to engineer a devaluation of the dollar in terms of other currencies. It could not do so easily, because of the institutional arrangements that had developed under the Bretton Woods System. Exchange rates for the dollar were maintained by other governments, whose interventions kept their dollar rates close to their parities, and a change in the dollar price of gold would not do the trick, because other governments could nullify its practical effect by changing the par values of their currencies to keep their dollar rates unchanged.

The United States had to disrupt those arrangements to achieve its new objective, and that is what happened in August 1971, when President Nixon suspended US gold sales, imposed a 10 per cent surcharge on imports, and left the rest to John Connally, his Secretary of the Treasury. Exchange-rate policies clashed decisively, and the conflict had to be resolved by negotiation. The process took four months and culminated in the Smithsonian Agreement, the only instance of a global exchange-rate realignment.[8]

In an odd sort of way, governments had come full circle, from collective management through the IMF, agreed at Bretton Woods but never implemented, to collective management directly by governments. But this regime was not to last. The Smithsonian Agreement began to unravel. The pound was allowed to float downward in June 1972 and the Swiss franc to float upward in January 1973, and everything else came unstuck one month later, when the United States tried to engineer a second devaluation of the

12

dollar. The Japanese authorities responded immediately by allowing the yen to float upward; the German authorities followed two weeks later in the face of massive capital inflows, and they were joined by other European countries.

We cannot know what governments had in mind for the long run – how many officials truly favoured a shift to floating exchange rates. Recollections are not very helpful, because most of us have perfect foresight after the event. There had been an important change in the United States. George Shultz had replaced John Connally as Secretary of the Treasury, and Shultz favoured floating rates. Yet governments continued with the task they had begun shortly before the float began, when they had established the Committee of Twenty to remodel the Bretton Woods System.[9]

Whenever the next attempt is made to reform the monetary system, participants should look very closely at that last one. There were tactical mistakes that eroded political support for the work of the Committee. There was too much concern with methods and mechanics and too little concern with the need to reconcile the very different meanings that governments attached to their common objective – designing a more symmetrical monetary system.[10] For the major European participants, this meant reducing the role of the dollar in order to reduce their vulnerability to US policies and to subject the United States to the same balance-of-payments discipline that other countries faced. They would have the same objective today. For the United States, symmetry meant more freedom to alter its exchange rate, the option that had always been available to other countries when the balance-of-payments constraint became too onerous. It could not accept a new regime that might force it to adopt disruptive tactics, as it did in August 1971. And it would likewise have the same objective today.

The Committee of Twenty continued its work for more than a year after the collapse of the Smithsonian Agreement. With the advent of the first oil crisis, however, governments concluded that it would be impossible to peg exchange rates and turned to the ratification of the new regime. At the Rambouillet Summit in November 1975, an artful agreement between France and the United States endorsed a 'stable system' of exchange rates, rather than exchange-rate stability itself. Two months later, the IMF Interim Committee agreed to a comprehensive revision of the Fund's Articles of Agreement. The same artful language appeared in

the new version of Article IV, defining the obligations of governments with regard to exchange rates. Its principal provisions are
reproduced in Figure 2.1. The old obligation to propose par values
to the Fund was replaced by the requirement in Section 2(a) that
members keep the Fund informed about their exchange-rate
arrangements. The need for Fund approval of changes in par values
was replaced by the requirement in Section 3(b) that the Fund
'exercise firm surveillance' over its members' exchange-rate policies.

There was a good deal of intervention during the early years of
floating, and the IMF's *Guidelines for Surveillance*, adopted to
implement Article IV, endorsed the use of intervention to combat
'disorderly' conditions in foreign-exchange markets. Nevertheless,
the Fund warned against sustained intervention or the use of trade
and capital controls to 'manipulate' exchange rates, and there was a
discernible shift in official sentiment away from 'dirty' to 'clean'
floating. The solution of the *N*th country problem would be left to
the foreign-exchange market.

In November 1978, the US, German, and Japanese authorities
had intervened heavily to halt a depreciation of the dollar. In 1979
and 1980, the US authorities had intervened on the other side of the
market to slow down the subsequent appreciation, and the United
States began to acquire sizeable foreign-exchange reserves. Soon
after taking office, however, the Reagan administration halted all
such acquisitions, saying that it would not need reserves because it
would not intervene to influence exchange rates. And other con-
servative governments took similar, if somewhat more guarded,
positions. The Versailles Summit of 1982 established a working
group to study the role of intervention, and its report was predict-
ably critical of using intervention for exchange-rate management.
Intervention could play a useful but limited role in certain circumstances, but mainly to draw the markets' attention to the implica-
tions of monetary policies. It could not and should not be used to
resist market forces (Working Group, 1983).

The same view was expressed in a second, more comprehensive,
report on the monetary system commissioned by the Williamsburg
Summit in 1983. It worried about the volatility of floating rates and
warned that 'large movements in real exchange rates may lead to
patterns of international transactions that are unlikely to be sustainable', but it laid most of the blame for exchange-rate instability on
'inadequate and inconsistent policies that have led to divergent

Figure 2.1 The ratification of floating exchange rates

Article IV
Obligations regarding exchange arrangements

Section 1. General obligations of members

Recognizing that the essential purpose of the international monetary system is to provide a framework that facilitates the exchange of goods, services, and capital . . . and that a principal objective is the continuing development of the orderly underlying conditions that are necessary for financial and economic stability, each member undertakes to collaborate with the Fund and other members to assure orderly exchange arrangements and to promote a stable system of exchange rates. In particular, each member shall: (i) endeavor to direct its economic and financial policies toward the objective of fostering orderly economic growth with reasonable price stability, with due regard for circumstances; (ii) seek to promote stability by fostering orderly underlying economic and financial conditions and a monetary system that does not tend to produce erratic disruptions; (iii) avoid manipulating exchange rates or the international monetary system in order to prevent effective balance of payments adjustment or to gain an unfair competitive advantage over other members . . .

Section 2. General exchange arrangements

(a) Each member shall notify the Fund . . . of the exchange arrangements it intends to apply in fulfillment of its obligations under Section 1 of this Article, and shall notify the Fund promptly of any changes in its exchange arrangements.

(b) Under an international monetary system of the kind prevailing on January 1, 1976, exchange arrangements may include (i) the maintenance by a member of a value for its currency in terms of the special drawing right or another denominator, other than gold, selected by the member, or (ii) cooperative arrangements by which members maintain the value of their currencies in relation to the value of the currency or currencies of other members, or (iii) other exchange arrangements of a member's choice. . . .

Section 3. Surveillance over exchange arrangements

(a) The Fund shall oversee the international monetary system in order to ensure its effective operation, and shall oversee the compliance of each member with its obligations under Section 1 of this Article.

(b) In order to fulfill its functions under (a) above, the Fund shall exercise firm surveillance over the exchange rate policies of members, and shall adopt specific principles for the guidance of all members with respect to those policies. . . .

economic performance' (Deputies, 1985, paras. 17, 20). In effect, officials endorsed the view then prevalent among economists that foreign-exchange markets absorb information efficiently and should not be blamed for the policies on which they are passing judgment. That would be shooting the messenger who brings embarrassing news (Frenkel, 1987).

A few short months later, however, governments took a different view. On 22 September 1985, in the Plaza Communiqué, they sent the messenger back to the market to say that the market was not doing its job:

> The Ministers and Governors agreed that exchange rates should play a role in adjusting external imbalances. In order to do this, exchange rates should better reflect fundamental economic conditions than has been the case. They believe that agreed policy actions must be implemented and reinforced to improve the fundamentals further, and that in view of the present and prospective changes in fundamentals, some further orderly appreciation of the main non-dollar currencies against the dollar is desirable. They stand ready to cooperate more closely to encourage this when to do so would be helpful.

And they took the next step in the Louvre Accord of 22 February 1987:

> The Ministers and Governors agreed that the substantial exchange-rate changes since the Plaza Agreement will increasingly contribute to reducing external imbalances and have now brought their currencies within ranges broadly consistent with underlying economic fundamentals, given the policy commitments summarized [earlier] in this statement.
>
> Further substantial exchange-rate shifts among their currencies could damage growth and adjustment prospects in their countries.
>
> In current circumstances, therefore, they agreed to cooperate closely to foster stability of exchange rates around current levels.

And so full circle once again, from the Smithsonian to the Louvre and from respectful acceptance of the markets' views to a new attempt at collective management. The results are examined later in this paper.

The arguments for exchange-rate management

Economists like to believe that they influence policies. Those who favour floating rates would like to think that governments were listening in 1973. Those who favour managed rates would like to think that governments were listening in 1985. The truth is more complicated.

The move to floating rates in 1973 was a ragged retreat in the face of market forces. In the key case of Germany, for example, the authorities had to choose between two distasteful prospects. An appreciation of the mark would repel inflationary pressures coming from abroad but would weaken the competitive position of German industry, while further intervention to support the dollar would raise the money supply and intensify domestic inflationary pressures. Their strong aversion to inflation led the Germans to abandon their exchange-rate target in order to defend their money-supply target, and they have made the same choice many times since.

The subsequent decision to ratify floating rates also reflected practical considerations – how hard it would be to choose and defend a new set of pegged exchange rates under conditions prevailing in the mid-1970s, when growth rates and inflation rates differed widely across countries. That decision, however, was made somewhat easier by the economists' prediction that governments would have more freedom to pursue independent policies, and the influence of free-market monetarism on academic and official thinking helps to explain the subsequent move to freer floating in the early 1980s.

The recent revival of interest in exchange-rate management must likewise be explained by practical concerns rather than the influence of economic arguments.

The Plaza Communiqué of 1985, which sent the messenger back to the market, was inspired by concerns about protectionism in the United States. The strong dollar was stimulating US imports and depressing exports, and the Reagan administration was far from certain that it could block the passage of flagrantly restrictive trade legislation. In the statements of national policy aims appended to the Plaza Communiqué, each government pledged itself to resist protectionism.

The more ambitious Louvre Accord of 1987 reflected urgent problems in Japan and Europe. The depreciation of the dollar in the wake of the Plaza Agreement was worrying Japanese industry and had already produced a bilateral agreement between Washington and Tokyo, using language echoed later in the Louvre Accord. In Europe, the falling dollar was seen to be producing serious tensions within the EMS, which tied the French franc and Italian lira to the rising German mark. Those tensions had already forced one realignment of EMS exchange rates in January 1987, and European governments wanted to avoid another. The Louvre Accord allayed these concerns by committing the United States to collaborate closely with the Japanese and Europeans in keeping the dollar from falling further.[11]

Nevertheless, the Louvre Accord and subsequent events have focused the attention of officials and economists on the basic arguments for exchange-rate management and the broader problems of policy coordination. The two main arguments for managing exchange rates were set out briefly at the start of this chapter. One is based on views about political behaviour; the other, on views about market behaviour.

The simplest form of the political argument is the assertion that governments cannot be trusted to pursue sensible or predictable policies. They must be bound by rules. When the argument is put that way, it is unappealing to politicians, who want to know how rules can help them rather than constrain them. For this same reason, incidentally, European advocates of pegged exchange rates damage their own case by dwelling on the need to constrain or discipline the United States – the argument for symmetry made by Europeans in the Committee of Twenty.[12]

When put somewhat differently, however, the political argument can be appealing even to politicians. A case can be made for tying one's own hands in order to purchase credibility – for adopting a strict rule to persuade the public (and other politicians) that an unpopular or painful policy will not be abandoned. Some central banks adopted money-supply rules for that pragmatic reason rather than great faith in the long-term economic benefit of fixing the growth rate for some monetary aggregate. Some European governments saw the same advantage in joining the EMS. By pegging their currencies to the German mark, they linked their monetary policies to those of the Bundesbank

18

and thus borrowed some of its credibility as an implacable foe of inflation.[13]

This argument has only limited validity. Self-imposed rules tend to lose their force, and thus their influence on credibility, as soon as they come into conflict with other policy goals. The US commitment to a fixed price for gold began to lose its force long before it was renounced in 1971; it did not prevent the United States from pursuing domestic policies that led eventually to an unmanageable balance-of-payments problem. It may be objected that the United States succeeded for some time in relaxing the constraint imposed by the vestigial Bretton Woods version of the gold standard. It pressed other governments to accumulate dollars rather than convert them into gold. But that is precisely the point. The United States found ways to keep its promise about the gold price without honouring the purpose of that promise. To leap from the 1960s to the 1980s, can anyone truly believe that the Reagan administration would have forsworn its idiosyncratic fiscal experiment in 1981 had it been committed to a pegged exchange rate or, for that matter, been bound by the Balanced Budget Amendment that it has endorsed so often? Recall how vehemently it denied any connection between the US budget deficit and the behaviour of the dollar.

The case for rules is even weaker when made in its appealing, pragmatic form. When a rule is adopted primarily to enhance the credibility of a particular policy, it must start to lose its force as soon as the more basic policy goal begins to lose its urgency. The strength of the commitment to the EMS may be getting weaker in European countries that have started to question the cost of importing Germany's low growth rate along with its low inflation rate, which may in turn explain the sudden flurry of interest in establishing a European central bank to carry Europe forward from a set of pegged exchange rates to a common currency.[14] A self-imposed constraint can be quite useful, but only for as long as it is seen to serve the policy-maker's own purpose.

The economic argument for exchange-rate management is summed up by two statements early in this chapter. Those who 'produce' exchange rates in the foreign-exchange market are differently motivated from those who 'consume' them in the markets for goods, services, and long-term assets. Furthermore, exchange rates are very flexible, like other asset prices, whereas goods prices are sticky, so that nominal and real exchange rates move together.

A growing body of evidence supports the first assertion. Inhabitants of the foreign-exchange market have been shown to behave myopically, even irrationally,[15] and this would be reason enough to challenge the conventional wisdom of the early 1980s, which held that markets are wiser than governments. But the second assertion is more important. If goods prices were perfectly flexible, there would be little cause to worry about exchange-rate arrangements. Goods markets would optimize relative prices instantaneously, including real exchange rates, even if they had to cope with nonsensical messages from the foreign-exchange market. Governments could then stabilize their money stocks and let the foreign-exchange market determine nominal exchange rates, or could peg exchange rates and let the market determine national money stocks. It is therefore the stickiness of goods prices that makes the exchange-rate regime important. When nominal exchange rates affect real rates, they also affect economic activity – its level, location, and composition.[16]

The strength of the connection between nominal and real exchange rates is shown clearly in Figure 2.2, which draws attention sharply to the huge swing in real rates that occurred in the 1980s. This may have been the most expensive round trip in recent history, save perhaps for the big swing in oil prices that began and ended earlier. It would have been very expensive if the effects of the strong dollar had been fully reversed when the exchange-rate movement was reversed. But the costs of the swing have been even bigger, because its effects will never be reversed completely.

Whole industries and regions in the United States have been affected permanently, because plants that were shut down when they became uncompetitive will not be reopened. They were not inefficient in 1980 but have been rendered obsolete by decisions and events taken in response to the swing in the real exchange rate. Export and domestic markets have been lost to foreign competitors, who invested heavily to capture them initially and will not give them up, even though they are not as profitable now.[17] This is not a mercantilistic dirge. It is a lament for wasted resources – for the physical and human capital that has been misallocated, not only in the United States but in the rest of the world as well.

These real resource costs were compounded by permanent damage to the trading system. Although it was strongly opposed to protectionism, the Reagan administration was unable to resist

Figure 2.2 Nominal and real effective exchange rates for US dollar, 1971–87

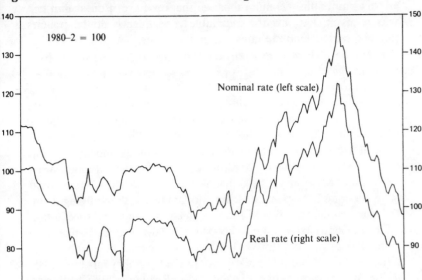

1980–2 = 100

Nominal rate (left scale)

Real rate (right scale)

Source: Morgan Guaranty Trust, *World Financial Markets,* various issues; includes currencies of 15 industrial countries weighted by bilateral trade in manufactures.

pressures from industries severely hurt by the appreciation of the dollar. It imposed new restrictions and tightened old ones on imports of automobiles, steel, textiles, and apparel, and many of them are still in place. Exchange-rate fluctuations tend to ratchet up trade barriers.

But was the whole trip necessary? Was the foreign-exchange market doing a job that other markets could not do because goods prices are not flexible enough? That is the key question.

Krugman (1988a) dismisses the question derisively, saying that there was no fundamental reason for raising the real value of the dollar in 1984 only to reduce it 1985. He argues persuasively that this particular segment of the whole round trip reflected irrational behaviour by the foreign-exchange market. It is harder, however, to blame the *whole* round trip on that sort of behaviour. The appreciation of the dollar began with the tightening of US monetary policy in 1979. It was driven thereafter by the capital inflow induced by the

21

combination of tight money with a large and growing budget deficit. In this simple but meaningful sense, the first part of the round trip was necessary. It was the inevitable consequence of the policies pursued by the United States.

How, then, *should* we apportion blame for the whole round trip? Some of the blame must be borne by the foreign-exchange market, not just for the speculative bubble of 1984–5 but for taking a typically myopic view two or three years earlier. If its inhabitants had been endowed with the marvellous attributes displayed by those who populate many economists' models, they would have known that the US budget and trade deficits could not last indefinitely and that the dollar would have to return eventually to something near its 1980 level. As soon as the dollar started to rise, then, they would have begun to bet against it, selling dollars rather than buying them. In other words, they would have engaged in stabilizing speculation on a sufficiently large scale to keep nominal and real exchange rates from changing significantly. (This argument would hold, moreover, if the capital inflow had been due not to the US policy mix but rather to the 'safe haven' motive invoked by the Reagan administration to defend its policies from those who blamed them for the rising dollar.)

The rest of the blame, however, must be borne by US policies or by the exchange-rate regime. It is tempting, of course, to blame US policies, which is what all right-thinking monetarists would have done if some had not been obliged to defend them. But that is to make the same mistake that we have made too often – to evaluate exchange-rate regimes under ideal policies. The lesson taught by the round trip of 1980–7 has to do with the high cost of imperfect policies under floating exchange rates – the point made earlier in different terms, that floating rates produce a peculiarly painful form of interdependence. It could have been illustrated just as vividly by the British experience of 1980–1, when the policies of the Thatcher government caused sterling to appreciate in nominal and real terms, with irreversible effects on Britain's economic landscape. There will be times, moreover, when the most sensible policies affect exchange rates in ways that are not essential or even helpful to the central purposes of those policies.

The core of the case for exchange-rate management is the sad but simple fact that ~~policies~~ and markets are imperfect and interact in costly ways under floating rates.

The case for exchange-rate management, however, cannot be made wholly by indirection – by showing that floating exchange rates have been more costly than their advocates or critics had predicted. Like democracy, a floating-rate regime could be worse than any other apart from those that might replace it. It is therefore necessary to examine the varieties of exchange-rate management that have been tried in the past or proposed for the future, not only to ask how costly they may be but also to examine the feasibility of exchange-rate management. That is the task ahead.

3

METHODS OF MANAGING EXCHANGE RATES

The range of possibilities

There are many ways to manage exchange rates. At one extreme, governments can try by word or deed to influence attitudes in the foreign-exchange market; as those efforts weaken in intensity and frequency, exchange rates float more freely. At the other extreme, exchange rates can be fixed unconditionally within a narrow band; as the fixing becomes more permanent and the band narrower, exchange-rate management approaches full-fledged currency unification.

Most methods of management, however, lie well within these two extremes. They involve conditional commitments to keep exchange rates within bands defined in relation to central or target rates, and they can be described by answering four questions:[1]

(1) How are the central rates chosen and changed, in order to locate and shift the bands?

(2) How firm and narrow are the bands?

(3) What policy instruments are used to keep rates within them?

(4) How much do markets know about the answers to the first three questions?

These questions can be answered independently, but some sets of answers do not add up sensibly. Answers to the second question, for example, affect answers to the third; when the bands are firm and narrow, official intervention must be used to keep market rates within them, because other policy instruments cannot do the job unaided. More important, answers to the fourth question rule out certain answers to the first and second; when the market is well informed about the governments' practices and plans, large shifts in narrow bands tend to provoke speculative pressures, which is why the Bretton Woods System became so brittle.

This chapter deals with the first three questions. The next chapter deals with the fourth and with the constraints it places on the adding up of answers. It argues that markets should be well informed and shows why this may mean that there can be no viable half-way house between freely floating and tightly managed rates. Before looking at the answers to the first three questions, however, let us look briefly at the main alternative to systematic management – the use of words or deeds to alter expectations and thus manage floating rates in an *ad hoc*, episodic manner.[2]

Episodic management

Many things that governments say and do can influence attitudes in the foreign-exchange market, as can expectations about future actions, whether well founded or not. From time to time, moreover, words and deeds are chosen with that as the main aim: to change the market's views about the outlook for exchange rates or the certainty with which it holds those views.

Economists tend to be sceptical about the effectiveness of these methods, because of their abiding faith in the quality of the information embodied in exchange rates. If markets are well informed and process information accurately, governments can affect exchange rates only by altering or promising to alter the fundamental economic conditions that determine exchange-rate behaviour in the long run.

In the monetary models of the 1970s, for example, the path of the exchange rate was determined primarily by relative rates of growth in national money supplies, and the market knew this. The words and deeds of governments were thus ineffective unless they supplied new information about those growth rates. In those models, for example, intervention could not influence exchange rates unless it affected the money supply or was deemed to convey information about the future of the money supply.*

But exchange rates depend on many fundamentals, not just money supplies, so governments have many ways to influence the market's views. Furthermore, the inhabitants of the foreign-exchange market have diverse objectives and different ways of processing new information. They disagree among themselves and hold their views with varying degrees of confidence. (If they held the same views and had the same objectives, they would want to take the same positions in the market, and the advent of new information would change exchange rates without changing those positions. There would be no need for trading. By implication, the vast amount of trading that actually occurs in foreign-exchange markets must testify to differences of view, although the views that matter most for the course of trading may have less to do with economic fundamentals than with traders' views about other traders' views – with average opinion now about average opinion an hour from now.)

In the real world, then, the words and deeds of governments *can* influence exchange rates. That is why Secretary Blumenthal's remarks were influential in June 1977, when the dollar began to depreciate, why policy announcements and intervention halted the depreciation in November 1978, and why the Plaza Agreement was influential in September 1985, when the dollar started to depreciate again.[3] It also explains why joint announcements and collective intervention tend to be more effective than unilateral words and deeds, and why intervention can be very effective when it is carefully timed, even when it is quite small compared with the huge turnover in the foreign-exchange market.

When governments give the appearance of being united and of holding their views firmly, while market participants are divided and uncertain, official pronouncements about exchange rates can have large effects, especially when backed by intervention or the threat of intervention, and intervention can be effective even when markets are sceptical about the governments' pronouncements.

---

*Ordinarily, intervention affects the money supply directly. When a central bank buys foreign currency, it pays by issuing a claim on itself and thus adds to the cash reserves of the banking system. To neutralize this impact on the money supply, the central bank must extinguish the newly created claim by selling domestic assets, such as government securities. This is *sterilized* intervention.

This was demonstrated dramatically early in January 1988, when the authorities halted a run on the dollar and turned it around sharply. Two weeks earlier, on 22 December, the G-7 governments had issued the second version of the Louvre Accord,[4] but the foreign-exchange market was not impressed. The dollar went on falling. Yet the market had reason to wonder how far the dollar would fall, because the US trade deficit appeared to be shrinking in response to the large depreciation that had already taken place. Average opinion predicted a further fall in the dollar, but evidence analysed in the appendix to this paper suggests that this expectation was not firmly held. The authorities were thus able to drive the market to cover by abrupt, concerted intervention at the start of January. The dollar rose and then stayed stable for many weeks.

In each of these three episodes, the authorities were unhappy with the actual or prospective level of exchange rates. Another approach to exchange-rate management attempts to maintain 'orderly markets' by using intervention to 'lean against the wind' and reduce the speed at which exchange rates are changing. Two quite different reasons have been given for following this strategy. The first appeals to the risk that rapidly changing rates are likely to produce speculative bubbles. The second appeals to the need for smoothing medium-term exchange-rate movements – for avoiding round trips in real exchange rates.

The first reason is weak analytically, because a rapidly changing exchange rate is apt to be the symptom of a speculative bubble rather than the cause. Furthermore, the beginning of a speculative bubble calls for the authorities to alter expectations by acting abruptly, as they did in January 1988, not to retreat slowly in the face of market pressures.

The second reason may be somewhat stronger analytically, although there are objections to it. There is the risk that 'leaning against the wind' will aggravate exchange-rate movements, because the market may interpret the intensity of intervention as a measure of the authorities' concern about the strength of the forces driving the exchange rate; it will then place its bets on a further movement of the rate rather than an early reversal.[5] The stronger the argument becomes, moreover, the stronger is the case for systematic management rather than episodic intervention – which brings us to the questions posed at the outset of this chapter.

27

Two caveats

There are two ways to answer those questions: by looking at various methods of exchange-rate management, historical and hypothetical, to ask how they answer them, or by looking at the questions, one by one, to explore the possibilities, and using the various methods of management as illustrations. The second approach is less tedious, but two warnings must be borne in mind.

First, we are dealing with exchange-rate arrangements for the large industrial countries, which have to be chosen and managed collectively, rather than arrangements for small countries, which can choose their exchange-rate regimes independently, without systemic consequences. (This distinction is breaking down, however, because the exchange-rate policies of certain developing countries, notably South Korea and Taiwan, have begun to have significant effects on the major countries. They were mentioned obliquely in the third version of the Louvre Accord – the G-7 Communiqué of April 1988.)

Second, an exchange-rate regime adds up to more than the sum of its technical characteristics, and it does not function in a vacuum. The early success and subsequent disintegration of the Bretton Woods System reflected the changing economic and political roles of the United States and the changing quality of US policies. The success of the European Monetary System has reflected the acceptability, if not the dominance, of German monetary policy and the political link between the EMS and the European Community.

The central rates

There are many ways to solve the technical problem of setting central rates. The value of each currency can be defined in terms of some outside asset such as gold, the method used originally in the IMF Articles of Agreement. It can be defined in terms of a common basket of currencies such as the Special Drawing Right (SDR) used by the IMF or the European Currency Unit (ECU) used by the EMS. It can be defined in terms of some national currency, whether or not a key currency in any other sense. These values can then be used to define a central rate for each pair of currencies, which locates the centre of the band for the bilateral exchange rate between them. And these techniques do not exhaust the possibilities. Instead of defining a central rate for each pair of currencies, Williamson (1985) would use the effective exchange rate for each national currency. This is a weighted average value of that country's currency in terms of all other important currencies, where 'importance' is defined by the impact of those currencies on the country's current-account balance.[6]

Williamson's system is simpler in one way, because there is just one band for each country's currency – the one that surrounds its effective rate. It is more complicated in other ways, because it is not symmetrical. The Canadian dollar and Mexican peso are more important for the US current account than for the German or Japanese, and changes in their values will alter the effective rate for the US dollar without having a comparable impact on the effective rates for the mark or yen. The asymmetry is not important in itself but can complicate the allocation of responsibilities among the governments involved in exchange-rate management.

If the Mexican peso appreciates in terms of all other currencies, the effective rate for the dollar will depreciate, but not those for the mark and yen. Therefore, the United States will be seen to bear the whole responsibility for keeping the dollar within its band. But the US policy response will alter the effective rates for the mark and yen and may thus lead to changes in German and Japanese policies. The dollar must be made to appreciate in terms of those currencies because it has depreciated in terms of the peso. As this happens, however, the effective rates for the mark and yen must start to depreciate. Hence, German and Japanese policies may have to change in parallel with US policies, rather than going in the opposite direction as they would in a fully symmetrical system.[7]

When a small number of major countries undertake to manage their exchange rates collectively, the framework for management should be designed symmetrically, in order to define obligations clearly and shut out extraneous complications.

A method for defining central rates is also a method for changing them. When one is chosen, so is the other. But the political and economic problems are far harder than the definitional problem.

The political problem is, of course, the old Nth country problem, and it has only one solution. Decisions about central rates must be made by governments, and unanimity must be the rule, as it is in the

EMS. Passivity is out of date, and supranationality is out of reach. Nevertheless, the IMF can play a useful role, much like the role it already plays in the multilateral surveillance of G-7 policies. It can supply the numbers and analysis needed for an orderly discussion among governments, and the Managing Director should not be excluded from the actual decision-making process.

The economic problem is easy to formulate. Central rates will not be viable for very long unless they are approximately equal to long-term equilibrium exchange rates. But what is the long-term equilibrium rate? When the question is put to governments, they make vague statements about the mutual compatibility of their policies and forecasts. When it is put to economists, they defer to the superior judgment of the market or retreat behind an answering volley of questions about hard analytical and normative issues.

The basic analytical issue is ignorance. Meese and Rogoff (1983) have shown decisively that simple econometric models cannot predict exchange rates. Frankel (1987a) has shown that large multi-country models disagree fundamentally about the behaviour of the world economy – about the sizes and even the signs of policy multipliers, which measure the effects of one country's policies on other economies, and about the sizes of changes in trade flows produced by changes in real exchange rates. This is the problem of model uncertainty that has been so heavily emphasized in recent discussions of policy coordination. Furthermore, new theoretical work suggests that small and large models alike may miss the mark completely by failing to allow for the irreversible nature of changes in trade patterns.[8]

The basic normative issue arises from two difficulties. The first has to do with domestic targets, the second with consistency in current-account targets.

Even if we had an acceptable model, showing how current-account balances respond to incomes, prices, and exchange rates, we could not compute equilibrium exchange rates without knowing what governments seek to achieve domestically – their targets for growth, employment, and inflation. In fact, we would need the consent of each government to every other government's aims. If Washington objected to the German growth rate and Bonn objected to the US inflation rate, both would object to the dollar/mark rate ground out by the model.

The problem of consistency would not arise in the absence of capital flows; each country's current-account balance would have to be zero. As soon as we admit those flows, however, current-account balances can differ from zero. It is therefore impossible to define equilibrium exchange rates without first defining an appropriate set of current-account balances, and the difficulty here becomes even clearer when the job is tackled from the other end – defining appropriate capital flows.

Those flows need not add up to zero for the particular subset of countries involved in exchange-rate management. But the net flow to or from the group must make sense from a global standpoint. It would not make sense right now, for example, if it implied a large net outflow to the less-developed countries, unless the developed countries were prepared to increase their lending. And capital flows *within* the group must make sense from two other perspectives. First, they must be sustainable over the medium term. Second, they must be broadly consistent with the monetary and fiscal policies that governments plan to pursue in the coming years. No one knows how to deal with these issues. Williamson has faced them frankly but has not satisfied his critics.[9]

This long list of problems would be daunting if governments were trying to fix exchange rates permanently. They may not be so serious in the present context – the search for a starting-point. It is less important for governments to be agreed and confident about the sustainability of the initial central rates than for them to reach agreement on two other matters – the policies that they should follow in order to validate those rates and the process they will use for altering the rates, not only to deal with new disturbances but also to correct mistakes in the initial settings. Criticism of the Louvre Accord has focused too heavily on the 'wrongness' of the rates that the G-7 governments chose to endorse. There has been too little criticism of the governments' failure to pursue domestic policies that might have made those rates sustainable and their apparent failure to adopt procedures for reviewing and revising their exchange-rate commitments in the light of new information.

It is instructive to recall the situation in 1979, when the EMS came into being. Inflation rates were high and different across Europe, and there were large differences in national policies (see Table 3.1). It would have been hard to choose a less auspicious year for setting central rates. But those rates were altered in the years that followed, more frequently than many had thought possible. There were four realignments in the first four years and three more in the next three years (see Table 3.2). Furthermore, governments adapted their policies to their exchange-rate commitments, and some of them used those commitments effectively to win domestic political support for the policies required to combat inflation. That is one reason for the diminishing frequency of EMS realignments.

Table 3.1 Economic indicators for EMS countries, 1979

Country	Inflation rate	Growth rate of money supply	Budget deficit as percentage of GDP
Belgium	4.5	2.5	7.6
Denmark	9.6	9.9	0.7
France	10.8	11.8	1.5
Germany	4.1	2.9	2.0
Ireland	13.2	8.1	11.9
Italy	14.8	23.7	10.2
Netherlands	4.2	2.8	4.6

Source: Inflation rates (consumer prices) and budget deficits (central governments) from International Monetary Fund, *International Financial Statistics*; growth rates of money supplies (narrow money) from Ungerer et al. (1986).

Table 3.2 Changes in EMS central rates

Currency	Sept. 1979	Nov. 1979	Mar. 1981	Oct. 1981	Feb. 1982	June 1982	Mar. 1983	July 1985	Apr. 1986	Aug. 1986	Jan. 1987
Belgian franc	0.0	0.0	0.0	0.0	−8.5	0.0	+1.5	+2.0	+1.0	0.0	+2.0
Danish kroner	−2.9	−4.8	0.0	0.0	−3.0	0.0	+2.5	+2.0	+1.0	0.0	0.0
German mark	+2.0	0.0	0.0	+5.5	0.0	+4.25	+5.5	+2.0	+3.0	0.0	+3.0
French franc	0.0	0.0	0.0	−3.0	0.0	−5.75	−2.5	+2.0	−3.0	0.0	0.0
Irish punt	0.0	0.0	0.0	0.0	0.0	0.0	−3.5	+2.0	0.0	−8.0	0.0
Italian lira	0.0	0.0	−6.0	−3.0	0.0	−2.75	−2.5	−6.0	0.0	0.0	0.0
Dutch guilder	0.0	0.0	0.0	+5.5	0.0	+4.25	+3.5	+2.0	+3.0	0.0	+3.0

Source: Ungerer et al. (1986) and Artis and Taylor (1988); appreciations (+) and depreciations (−) are the percentage changes against the group of currencies whose bilateral rates remained unchanged (except for the realignments of March 1983 and July 1985, involving all currencies, for which the percentages shown are those given in the official communiqués); the corresponding changes against the ECU are slightly different, because the value of the ECU is affected by each realignment.

There are no formal rules for realigning central rates in the EMS. The process is initiated whenever any member wants to change its rate.[10] But three special circumstances have helped to make the process work. (1) Because the EMS is linked to the EC, the threat to quit – and float – cannot be made easily. There has been hard bargaining about realignments, but no one has walked out. (2) An informal norm has been established gradually. Realignments may be sought only to offset losses of competitiveness – to bring a member's real rate back to what it was before – not to enhance competitiveness. This sets outer limits to the bargaining process. (3) The chronically strong mark has confronted the German authorities with the same dilemma that they have faced so often, and they have resolved it in the usual way, by letting the mark appreciate rather than letting the money supply rise. If they had opposed or delayed realignments, they would have forced their partners to borrow marks for intervention, which would have raised the German money supply.

A looser grouping of large countries – the United States, Japan, and Germany, for instance – might find it much more difficult to realign central rates frequently and speedily. There is intense commercial rivalry among them, and there is no global counterpart of the EC to discourage them from disrupting the negotiating process when they cannot get their way.

Would it perhaps be helpful to use 'objective indicators' to focus and structure the negotiating process? The possible candidates do not look promising.[11]

The equilibrium exchange rate would be the ideal indicator, because the central rate should change whenever it changes, and that is what Williamson proposes. But all of the issues discussed above get in the way of using it – the problem of model uncertainty, the need for mutual consent to domestic targets, and the very difficult problem of defining appropriate capital flows. It might thus be wise to use less contentious indicators – numbers that raise questions rather than numbers that purport to give answers.

The real exchange rate is one such number. If one country's prices rise more rapidly than others', its currency will have to depreciate eventually. That is the kernel of truth in the purchasing-power parity (PPP) doctrine and the basis for the norm adopted informally by the EMS. (It is likewise implicit in Williamson's proposal, because unwanted changes in effective real rates would be precluded by automatic changes in effective nominal rates.) But real exchange rates should not be held constant. They must be adjusted periodically to compensate for secular shifts in economic conditions. Otherwise, those shifts will make themselves felt in less acceptable ways, most notably and dangerously in mounting protectionist pressures.[12]

The current-account balance is bound to reflect some of the secular shifts that need to be offset by exchange-rate realignments. It is hard to use as an indicator, however, because it changes sharply in response to cyclical and other short-term forces but slowly in response to the real exchange rate itself. There are ways to adjust the raw numbers – to smooth away cyclical and transitory changes and update the influence of previous exchange-rate changes – but not without raising the same contentious issues that have to be resolved before one can compute equilibrium exchange rates.

Two other indicators – changes in reserves and changes in exchange rates – have been proposed from time to time.[13] Their usefulness depends in part on the characteristics of the exchange-rate regime. One with narrow and firm bands would stop a rate-based indicator from saying very much but would probably require enough intervention to make a reserve-based indicator useful. One with wide and soft bands would work the other way. But both of these indicators speak primarily to the recent state of play in the foreign-exchange market, which makes them rather redundant from the governments' standpoint. Governments already know what pressures they have faced. They need to know what pressures they are likely to face over the long term.

The bands
Under the Bretton Woods System, exchange rates were contained within narrow and hard bands. Until the Smithsonian Agreement of 1971, the spread was only 2 per cent; thereafter, it was 4.5 per cent. So too in the EMS, where the spread is likewise 4.5 per cent for six of the participating currencies and 12 per cent for the Italian lira. Under Williamson's target-zone proposal, by contrast, the bands would be wide and soft. Effective rates could change by 20 per cent, which means that any single bilateral rate could cross an even wider zone, and governments would not have to intervene when exchange rates reached the edges of their bands but would merely pledge to

Figure 3.1 The Williamson-Miller target-zone proposal

The Blueprint

The participating countries [the Group of Seven] agree that they will conduct their macroeconomic policies with a view to pursuing the following two intermediate targets:

(1) A rate of growth of domestic demand in each country calculated according to a formula designed to promote the fastest growth of output consistent with gradual reduction of inflation to an acceptable level and agreed adjustment of the current account of the balance of payments.

(2) A real effective exchange that will not deviate by more than [10] per cent from an internationally agreed estimate of the 'fundamental equilibrium exchange rate', the rate estimated to be consistent with simultaneous internal and external balance in the medium term.

To that end, the participants agree that they will modify their monetary and fiscal policies according to the following principles:

(A) The *average level* of world (real) short-term interest rates should be revised up (down) if aggregate growth of national income is threatening to exceed (fall short of) the sum of the target growth of nominal demand for the participating countries.

(B) *Differences* in short-term interest rates among countries should be revised when necessary to supplement intervention in the exchange markets to prevent the deviation of currencies from their target ranges.

(C) National *fiscal policies* should be revised with a view to achieving national target rates of growth of domestic demand.

The rules (A) to (C) should be constrained by the medium-term objective of maintaining the real interest rate in its historically normal range and of avoiding an increasing or excessive ratio of public debt to GNP.

Source: Williamson and Miller (1987), p. 2; brackets and italics in original.

guard against this possibility by making appropriate policy adjustments. The most recent version of that proposal is reproduced in Figure 3.1.[14]

The case for hard bands – for mandatory intervention to keep exchange rates from crossing the boundaries – is made in the next chapter. It is based on the need to anchor expectations in the foreign-exchange market. But hardness and narrowness need not go together, though that has been the normal practice. There is, in fact, a strong case for using fairly wide bands.

First, the exchange rate must have some leeway to participate in the balance-of-payments adjustment process. Admittedly, exchange-rate movements may have been more hurtful than helpful during the past few years, and modest movements may not make a major contribution. But they can be more helpful and more potent if exchange-rate expectations are more firmly anchored. They can be more helpful because they are less likely to be driven by extrapolative expectations. They can be more potent because the users of exchange rates, especially corporate planners, are less likely to discount the durability of exchange-rate movements.[15] The bands should not be wide enough to offset every shock or shift that needs to be neutralized by changing real exchange rates; large shocks can be handled by realigning central rates. And governments should not be allowed to procrastinate – to leave to the exchange rate the work that should be done by changing domestic policies. It is necessary to discipline governments as well as markets. But market-determined changes in exchange rates should not be suppressed completely.

Second, there is need to give governments some leeway. They need time to make and implement policy decisions and room to compromise among objectives. The rigidities and long lags in adjusting fiscal policies, not only in the United States but in other countries too, mean that monetary policies cannot be used exclusively for exchange-rate management. They have also to be used for demand management.[16] Furthermore, governments need room for manoeuvre in the foreign-exchange market. Although it is important to anchor expectations – for the market to know that governments mean what they say when they promise to prevent large exchange-rate swings – it is equally important for governments to have tactical flexibility. They must be able to surprise the market from time to time, as they did in January 1988, when they exploited and intensified uncertainty about the near-term outlook for exchange rates.

Third, the foreign-exchange market must not be invited to make one-way bets of the sort that provoked speculative crises under the Bretton Woods System:

> Each government accepted the obligation to defend a narrow band around a fixed [parity] until further notice, but reserved the right to change the parity. Those fixed rates periodically became disequilibrium rates ... either through real shocks or more typically through differential inflation. Since governments were supposed to maintain fixed parities except *in extremis*, they could hardly propose a parity change before it was obvious to

all that a change was necessary. But when the market came to realize that a change was needed, a switch out (in) offered the prospect of substantial overnight gains if the currency was devalued (revalued) and the central bank was obliged to buy (sell) back its foreign exchange reserves at a higher price than it had sold (bought) them, at negligible risk (because of the narrow band) if the parity was unchanged. This was the famous one-way bet. To offer speculators a one-way bet is indeed to give them a field day (Williamson and Miller, 1987, pp. 58–9).

There are two ways of shifting the odds against this possibility – by fostering uncertainty about the timing of realignments and by making the exchange-rate band wide enough to accommodate the realignments.

The first is hard but not impossible. There is no need for finance ministers to meet with ostentatious confidentiality. They need not meet at all. Telephones and scramblers are sufficient. It may even be possible to introduce an element of randomness into the timing of realignments. Exchange rates should not be moved around merely to make noise and confuse the market. Nevertheless, realignments should be undertaken before the need for them has become overwhelmingly clear, even at the risk of having to reverse them later.

The second task is easier in both principle and practice. Speculators can make one-way bets only when they know that a change in central rates will be large enough to drag market exchange rates with them. Suppose that the lira rests at the bottom of its 12 per cent EMS band. If it is devalued by more than 12 per cent, the top of the new band will lie below the bottom of the old one, which means that the market rate must move with the central rate, and those who have sold lire in anticipation of the devaluation will be able to buy them back at a lower price. If the lira is devalued by less than 12 per cent, however, the top of the new band will lie above the bottom of the old, and the market rate need not move at all. It can indeed be driven in the opposite direction, as those who sold lire before the devaluation begin to repurchase them. This is what is meant by making the band wide enough to accommodate realignments.[17]

Although the EMS bands are quite narrow, they have been wide enough to accommodate many of the realignments shown in Table 3.2. The record is reviewed in the appendix to this paper, which shows that the new and old bands overlapped in 70 per cent of all the cases in which realignments changed the bilateral bands and in 60 per cent of the narrow-band cases (i.e., excluding those involving the lira). Furthermore, bands as wide as those for the lira would have accommodated *all* of the realignments. The largest change shown in Table 3.2 was the 10 per cent devaluation of the French franc in terms of the mark, in June 1982. By contrast, all of the exchange-rate changes made by major industrial countries from 1950 through 1970 were bigger than the 4.5 per cent EMS band, and three were bigger than the 12 per cent band for the lira.[18]

The width of the band required to accommodate realignments is the quotient of two numbers: the rate of change in central rates required to avoid cumulative disequilibria and the frequency with which realignments can be made. Because it might be hard to realign the key exchange rates more than once a year, and changes in nominal exchange rates must be large enough to offset differences between inflation rates as well as real shocks and shifts, bands for the key currencies should not be narrower than 10 per cent. A larger number might be prudent but would be too big to anchor expectations.

The policy instruments

What policy instruments should governments use to keep exchange rates from leaving their bands? It is useful to begin with the old distinction between financing and adjustment. A country can finance a balance-of-payments deficit by using reserves or reserve credit; that is much the same as saying that it can intervene on the foreign-exchange market to stabilize its currency. Alternatively, it can eliminate the deficit by adjusting its macroeconomic policies or changing its exchange rate, or it can suppress the deficit by trade or capital controls.

There is a clear case for financing a temporary deficit; well-functioning markets would do this on their own under floating exchange rates and would thus stabilize the rates themselves. But that does not exhaust the issue. On the one hand, a government should not rely entirely on financing, even for a temporary deficit, if it cannot draw down its reserves without rebuilding them later. On the other hand, adjustment takes time, and the fastest path to long-run equilibrium may not be the best path when prices and wages are sticky. Adjustment and financing must go together.[19]

To complicate matters, a deficit can be financed by attracting private capital inflows rather than using reserves. Therefore, intervention and interest-rate policies can be used jointly to finance imbalances and thus stabilize exchange rates. That is the view taken in the Williamson-Miller *Blueprint* reproduced above as Figure 3.1. Intervention and interest-rate differences are assigned to keep effective exchange rates from leaving their bands, while the global average of real interest rates and national fiscal policies are assigned to control domestic demand. The successful control of domestic demand can be described as pre-emptive adjustment because it avoids inflations and recessions that would lead to external imbalances. The rest is left to exchange-rate changes. In the Williamson-Miller framework, these are made automatically to compensate for residual differences in national inflation rates, and automatic changes are supplemented by periodic realignments to keep effective central rates in line with long-run equilibrium rates.

The same basic approach is recommended by Meade (1984) and goes back to Mundell (1962). It is more sensible than the framework proposed by McKinnon (1988), who argues that fiscal policies should be used to regulate current-account balances, because real exchange rates do not affect them, that the global money supply should be used to control or anchor the global price level, and that intervention should be used to keep exchange rates at purchasing-power parity. Fiscal policies cannot control current-account balances without imposing unemployment on deficit countries and inflationary pressures on surplus countries. They may be needed to validate changes in real exchange rates but cannot replace them.[20]

While eminently sensible in principle, the Williamson-Miller framework raises two difficult issues. First, the instruments assigned to control domestic demand may be inadequate for that purpose and cannot be used without concern for their balance-of-payments effects. Second, the distinction between intervention and interest-rate or monetary policy may be drawn more sharply than warranted.

Although fiscal policies are not efficient instruments for controlling current-account balances, they do affect those balances. In fact, shifts in fiscal policies are among the hardest disturbances to neutralize by monetary and exchange-rate policies.[21] It would therefore be risky for governments to pursue independent fiscal policies, and a loosely defined domestic target may not constrain them sufficiently. This matter will come up again in Chapter 6, which examines the links between exchange-rate management and macro-economic policy coordination and argues that the multilateral surveillance of G-7 policies should focus intensively on their fiscal policies.

Furthermore, fiscal policies are too cumbersome to control domestic demand completely. Even when they are part of the solution, not part of the problem, they cannot do the whole job. Monetary policies have to be used too, not just to regulate the average interest rate, as in the Williamson-Miller framework, but to set the appropriate interest rate for each country. From time to time, moreover, interest-rate policies must be modified to deal with financial crises; that is what happened at the start of the debt crisis in 1982 and after the stock-market crash in 1987. This means, in turn, that interest-rate policies cannot be used exclusively to regulate exchange rates, and more must be done by intervention.

This brings us directly to the second issue. If foreign and domestic assets are very close substitutes, governments may not have enough independent policy instruments to pursue exchange-rate stability and manage aggregate demand simultaneously. The point is usually made in different form. When foreign and domestic assets are very close substitutes, sterilized intervention is ineffective; a central-bank transaction in foreign currencies cannot have different exchange-rate effects from a central-bank transaction in domestic bonds, so one will cancel the other. Under those conditions, moreover, interest rates are tied tightly together. They cannot be adjusted independently to manage domestic demand.

What do we know about the degree of substitutability among assets denominated in different currencies? The evidence is inconclusive. If assets were perfect substitutes and asset holders had rational expectations, the foreign-exchange market would be efficient in the finance-theoretic sense; the forward rate would be the best predictor of the future spot rate. Econometric evidence rejects this view.[22] But that does not settle the matter. It may merely say that expectations are not rational or that the rationality of expectations cannot be represented in the conventional way, by using the actual exchange rate to stand for the expected rate.[23] Evidence concerning the effectiveness of sterilized intervention is likewise inconclusive. Simulations have shown that it is less effective than non-sterilized intervention,[24] and Rogoff (1984) has found that sterilized intervention does not have any effect on exchange rates, but his results are contradicted by several other studies.[25]

The debate is not over, and it is equally appropriate to criticize policy recommendations that depend heavily on the effectiveness of sterilized intervention and those that depend on the limiting assumption of perfect substitutability. Nevertheless, one point is clear. Even if foreign and domestic assets are very close substitutes, intervention may be the most effective way of defending hard margins. There are two reasons.

First, it is impossible to know in advance the size of the open-market operation required to achieve a given result in the foreign-exchange market. Intervention at the margin, by contrast, is a price-fixing strategy that makes it unnecessary to worry about quantities, which become endogenous. Second, the transmission of events from one market to another does not take place instantaneously, which means that a well-calculated open-market operation in the domestic bond market may not have an immediate, one-to-one effect in the foreign-exchange market, even when it should have this effect on average.

All arrangements involving hard bands necessitate intervention. They can differ only in the ways that they assign or divide responsibility among the participating countries. Those differences are not unimportant, however, when combined with other institutional features of the monetary system. These matters will come up again in Chapter 5.

4
GOVERNMENTS AND MARKETS

Introduction

The preceding chapter began with four questions and examined the first three, on setting and changing central rates, the width and hardness of the bands around them, and the merits of various policies that might be used to defend them. It stressed the need for frequent realignments and for bands sufficiently wide to accommodate those realignments. It argued that hard bands would have to be defended by intervention, not merely by interest-rate policies, and that interest-rate policies cannot be used exclusively for managing exchange rates, because fiscal policies are too rigid to stabilize aggregate demand.

This chapter examines the fourth question, but divides it into positive and normative questions: How much *can* the market know about the targets and instruments of exchange-rate management? How much *should* the market know? The normative question is fundamental. It is another way of asking whether governments can manage exchange rates by imprecise, private understandings among themselves or must adopt and publicize more formal rules.

Let us begin by recalling the main reason for raising these questions. Floating exchange rates have been more costly than expected because they have produced large changes in real exchange rates, which have in turn produced large changes in output and trade patterns and intensified protectionism. These effects are not fully reversed when exchange-rate movements are reversed. Accordingly, exchange-rate stability has become an important objective in its own right, not merely the incidental reward for following good policies. But stability cannot be achieved merely by endorsing it. Someone must act differently. The questions examined in Chapter 3 were concerned with changing behaviour by governments. The questions examined in this chapter are concerned with changing behaviour by markets.

Clearly, success in this second task depends on success in the first. Markets will not behave differently unless they believe that governments will do so. The problem is more complicated, however, because market participants are watching each other as well as watching governments, and they focus on near-term prospects for exchange rates rather than long-term prospects for policies. To modify market behaviour, then, governments must state their objectives clearly and pursue them by methods that are seen to affect exchange rates promptly and decisively. Interest-rate policies, for example, may be less effective than intervention, because their effects on exchange rates may not be prompt or decisive enough, but promises to intervene will not modify market behaviour unless they are backed by adequate reserves.

Commitment, credibility, and predictability

Issues of the sort examined in this chapter have played a major role in modern macroeconomic theory. Much attention has been paid to the need for predictable policies and the related problems of commitment and credibility.[1]

Strong results have been obtained using stylized models in which the sequence of events is crucial. Consider the framework used by Barro and Gordon (1983), in which wages and prices are set by the private sector in light of its expectations concerning the inflation rate, which depend in turn on its expectations concerning the money supply.

Suppose that the government promises to raise the money supply at a particular rate and that the private sector expects the government to keep its word. Wages and prices will be set accordingly, determining the actual inflation rate. At this point, the government has two options. If it keeps its promise, it will exactly validate the actual inflation rate, and there will be no change in output or employment. If it breaks its promise and raises the money supply faster, it will stimulate output and employment, because the actual inflation rate cannot change immediately. If it breaks its word frequently, however, it will lose credibility. The private sector will cease to pay attention to the government's promises; it will start to base its expectations on the rapid growth of the money supply that the government has been delivering rather than the low growth that it has been promising. The inflation rate will rise, and the rapid growth of the money supply will serve merely to validate the higher inflation rate. It will no longer stimulate output and employment.[2]

In this particular example and a larger class of models, the government is punished for trying to 'surprise' the private sector. It loses its reputation for making credible promises and is stuck with a higher inflation rate. But a government cannot make perfectly credible promises. It is sovereign and cannot precommit itself irrevocably. It can try to tie its own hands but cannot be kept from untying them. To acquire a good reputation for keeping its word, it must forswear temptation completely by refusing to make any promise that can generate conditions in which it will want to break its word.[3]

The force of this argument, however, depends on three assumptions. (1) The economic environment is one in which the private sector makes binding bargains about wages and prices, or other irrevocable commitments. (2) The government can and should make promises about its own behaviour, to facilitate planning by the private sector. (3) The 'game' played by the government vis-à-vis the private sector is the only game in town.

The assumption about binding bargains is unexceptional. In fact, the resulting stickiness of wages and prices is the central reason for wanting to stabilize nominal exchange rates. If wages and prices were completely flexible, nominal and real rates would not move together. But this sort of stickiness does not prevail in financial and foreign-exchange markets, where commitments can be covered or reversed instantaneously. It is the volatility of private behaviour, not its rigidity, that poses the main problem for exchange-rate management.

The case for predictable behaviour by governments is equally hard to challenge but has to be carefully qualified. First, governments should not promise more than they can safely expect to deliver. They should not court the risk of involuntary reneging.[4]

Second, governments may need to keep markets guessing by creating uncertainty about their tactics. This need for tactical flexibility is not necessarily incompatible with the need for predictable policies over the medium term. It is possible to pursue a stable course in respect of the money supply, for example, without telling the bond market in advance the precise size and timing of open-market operations, or to pursue exchange-rate stability without telling the foreign-exchange market when there will be intramarginal intervention. Furthermore, governments cannot be rigidly predictable in an uncertain world. If they were the only source of uncertainty facing the private sector, they could provide economic stability by following perfectly predictable policies. When governments and the private sector are *both* plagued by uncertainties, perfectly predictable policies can cause instability. A doggedly determined effort to follow such policies despite an unexpected change in circumstances will undermine a government's reputation for good sense more surely than a change in policy will undermine its reputation for good faith. A commitment to exchange-rate stability, for example, should not ossify into a rigid commitment to exchange-rate fixity. Real exchange rates must change when unexpected shocks or trends alter the underlying economic situation, and realignments of nominal rates may be the best way to change them.[5]

In the Barro-Gordon model, there is just one game going on: the government makes promises to influence the private sector. Therefore, the government cannot be punished severely for failing to keep its word. At worst, it can lose its ability to talk down the inflation rate. In practice, the government plays many games simultaneously, including the all-important political game. If it starts to cheat on any other player, all of them can punish it. In fact, they can choose a new government at the next election. The inconstancy of democratic politics is often cited as a reason for distrusting a government's promises; it cannot bind its successor. But the democratic process may work the other way, because every government wants to be its own successor. (Furthermore, a newly elected government will want to earn a reputation for reliability and is likely to honour inherited commitments unless they are fundamentally inconsistent with its basic aims.)

In the international context, moreover, governments can commit themselves more firmly, because the costs of cheating are higher. A government can hope to surprise the private sector from time to time without damaging its reputation. It cannot renege on its promises to other governments without impairing its ability to make more bargains with them. This is particularly important for the governments of the major industrial countries, because they must collaborate in many matters. They need to maintain their credibility to cooperate not merely in exchange-rate management, but in other economic, political, and strategic domains.

My earlier warnings about self-imposed rules continue to apply, even to rules adopted collectively. The rules will start to lose their force when policy objectives change, because governments will have less incentive to uphold them. But they will be more durable when they are multilateral, because governments must agree to loosen or abandon them, and they are less likely to abuse them by springing collective surprises on the private sector. They will be held back by the government least willing to ruin its reputation for keeping its promises to its own citizens.

What markets have known

Bearing these issues and arguments in mind, let us examine four models of exchange-rate management, to see how they have handled the problem of predictability. What have markets known about the governments' rules?

Under the Bretton Woods System, the market knew the parities or central rates, the width of the band around them, and the nature of the governments' commitment to defend them. The edges of the band were hard, and intervention was thus mandatory. The market did not know whether governments would engage in intramarginal intervention. It did not know when central rates would be realigned. But it came to learn that changes in central rates would be postponed for as long as possible and that they would be large compared with the width of the band, allowing the market to make one-way bets. Experience also taught the market to distrust official promises that exchange rates would not change.

The answers are the same under the European Monetary System, but the lessons of experience are rather different. Realignments have been smaller and more frequent and have been harder to forecast, because they have not always been triggered by speculative pressures the market's one-way bets. In fact, the realignment of January 1987 is the only one usually cited as having been driven mainly by speculative pressures.[6]

Under the Louvre Accord of 1987, markets knew nothing more than the authorities told them in the Communiqué – that nominal exchange rates prevailing at the time were broadly consistent with the 'fundamentals' and that the authorities would endeavour to stabilize them for as long as they continued to be consistent with the underlying situation. The market did not know the width of the band, which means that it could not know how hard the margins were or the methods that governments would use to defend them. But the market came to attach much more precision to the Louvre Accord. It claimed to know the central rates and the bands around them, and that the bands were rather hard.[7] The Louvre Accord was seen as a target-zone arrangement with narrow bands and all but mandatory intervention. When market commentary began to question the durability of the Louvre Accord, it was talking about these arrangements, and governments did not reject or try to amend the market's interpretation.[8]

The market would not know much more under Williamson's target-zone proposal than under the Louvre Accord. It would know the central rate and band for each effective rate, but there would be no central rate or band for any bilateral rate. And it would not be much help to know the bands for the effective rates, because they would be soft. Intervention would not be mandatory. The market would know somewhat more about realignments, since these would occur automatically to offset national inflation rates. But it could not predict the additional realignments aimed at altering real exchange rates. We cannot know what the market might learn from experience, but it would surely try to discover how governments interpreted their obligations – the softness of the bands in practice and the tightness of the governments' commitment to coordinate interest-rate policies.

The EMS rules are far more transparent than those of the Louvre Accord and those proposed by Williamson, and it might be possible to make them even clearer by telling the market more about realignments. Central rates might be realigned at regularly stated intervals to offset differences in national inflation rates. Some governments have done this from time to time, and a few have gone much further. They have announced in advance a schedule of small devaluations with a view to stabilizing expectations about the outlook for inflation. But these experiments have not been very successful, because the governments have tended to underestimate the inertial or self-perpetuating character of the inflationary process. Their currencies have become increasingly overvalued, and they have been compelled to abandon their plans and devalue their currencies sharply.

What markets should know

Experience under the Louvre Accord illustrates vividly the problems of trying to manage exchange rates by imprecise, opaque arrangements. Criticism of those arrangements has focused chiefly on the 'wrongness' of the central rates and the 'breakdown' of policy coordination.[9] Both objections are partly valid but neglect the other important defect of the Louvre Accord.

By the time of the Louvre Accord, the depreciation of the dollar had reversed most of the earlier appreciation. Yet many economists thought that the dollar should fall further to eliminate the US current-account deficit (and some continued to take that view in 1988, despite the additional depreciation after the October stock-market crash). But this does not condemn the Louvre Accord. Recall the point made in Chapter 3 about the economic situation in 1979, when the EMS came into being. There were strong reasons for believing that the initial exchange rates would have to change, and that is what happened thereafter. The EMS proved to be viable because the member governments developed procedures for realigning central rates in a timely way.

One realignment appears to have taken place under the Louvre Accord: the yen/dollar rate was 'rebased' in April 1987, after it had left the band chosen in February.[10] But the peculiar conditions that led to the Louvre Accord militated against flexibility. It came into being because governments were trying to persuade the market that there was no immediate need for the dollar to fall further, and the governments' quest for credibility locked them into an excessively rigid stance. This risk attends any agreement to stabilize exchange rates. The dynamics of the game between governments and markets invites confusion between the defence of the basic policy objective and the defence of particular rates. When governments review their exchange-rate commitments, they must be prepared to ask how soon central rates should change, not ask how long they can keep them from changing.

The exchange rates prevailing early in 1987 might have been sustainable had they been supported by changes in domestic policies

– a large cut in the US budget deficit matched in part by German and Japanese measures to stimulate aggregate demand. Performance fell short of these objectives, but the shortfall did not constitute a breakdown of policy coordination. Governments did not renege on their promises. They failed to promise enough. The policy commitments in the Louvre Accord were not new or more ambitious than those that the governments had made before, collectively and unilaterally. Figure 4.1 compares them with the declarations made much earlier in the Plaza Communiqué. They are not very different, save in the Japanese case.

More ambitious policy changes might have made it possible to stabilize exchange rates in 1987. Conversely, changes in exchange rates would have made it less important for governments to alter their policies. But the Louvre Accord was in jeopardy from the start because it was not transparent enough. The governments tried to conserve their credibility by being deliberately vague and avoiding commitments they might not be able to honour, and that was the right way to start. Nevertheless, they courted two other risks.

On the one hand, imprecise commitments like those in the Louvre Accord lead to disagreements among the governments themselves, which undermine the market's confidence in the governments' commitments. That is what happened in October 1987, on the eve of the stock-market crash, when the US Secretary of the Treasury, James Baker, objected bluntly to an increase in German interest rates. On the other hand, imprecise agreements tempt the market to draw up its own version of the rules, then to test the governments' commitment to them. When the governments fail to behave as expected, the market does not revise its own inferential version of the rules. It accuses the governments of backing down.

Williamson's target-zone proposal is open to the same objection. The bands are not well designed to stabilize exchange-rate expectations, and they are too wide for that purpose. The market is concerned with bilateral exchange rates, not with effective rates. And the bands are too soft to discourage the market from testing the governments' intentions.

Those who believe that markets are capable of taking a long view and processing new information efficiently criticize the Louvre Accord for being too vague about monetary and fiscal policies, not about the width and hardness of the bands. They might therefore

Figure 4.1 Declarations on Fiscal Policies in the Plaza Communiqué and Louvre Accord

The Plaza Communiqué (22 September 1985)

The United States Government will ... [continue] efforts to reduce government expenditures as a share of GNP in order to reduce the fiscal deficit ... [and implement] fully the deficit reduction package for fiscal year 1986. This package ... will not only reduce by over 1 per cent of GNP the budget deficit for FY 1986, but lay the basis for further significant reductions in the deficit ...

The ... German economy is already embarked on a course of steady economic recovery based increasingly on internally generated growth ... The priority objective of fiscal policy is to encourage private initiative and productive investments and maintain price stability ... [The] Federal Government will continue to reduce progressively the share of the public sector in the economy through maintaining firm expenditure control. The tax cuts due to take effect in 1986 and 1988 form part of the ongoing process of tax reform and reduction which ... will continue in a medium-term framework.

The ... Japanese economy is in an autonomous expansion phase mainly supported by domestic private demand increase ... Fiscal policy will continue to focus on the twin goals of reducing the central government deficit and providing a pro-growth environment for the private sector.

The Louvre Accord (22 February 1987)

The United States Government will pursue policies with a view to reducing the fiscal 1988 deficit to 2.3 per cent of GNP from its estimated level of 3.9 per cent in fiscal 1987 ... [The] growth in Government expenditures will be held to less than 1 per cent in fiscal 1988 as part of the continuing program to reduce the share of Government in GNP ...

The Government of the Federal Republic ... will pursue policies to diminish further the share of public expenditures in the economy and to reduce the tax burden ... with a comprehensive tax reform aimed at reinforcing the incentives for private-sector activity and investment. ... In addition, the Government will propose to increase the size of the tax reductions already enacted for 1988.

The Government of Japan will follow monetary and fiscal policies which will help to expand domestic demand and thereby continue to reduce the domestic [sic] surplus. The comprehensive tax reform, now before the Diet, will give additional stimulus to the vitality of the Japanese economy. ... A comprehensive economic program will be prepared after the approval of the 1987 budget by the Diet, so as to stimulate domestic demand ...

endorse the Williamson-Miller framework, which is not particularly clear about the governments' obligations concerning intervention but fairly explicit about their policy obligations. Yet markets have not been very good at taking a long view, and they might have other troubles with the Williamson-Miller framework. Lags in the policy-making process are bound to obscure the strength of the governments' commitment to it, and the obscurity would be compounded by the shortage of policy instruments emphasized in Chapter 3; governments must compromise among objectives rather than assign each policy instrument to a clearly defined policy target.

Rules for the conduct of monetary and fiscal policies cannot influence exchange-rate expectations decisively. What governments promise to do in the foreign-exchange market may be more influential than what they promise to do about interest rates or tax rates. The reaffirmation of the Louvre Accord in December 1987, after the stock-market crash, contributed less to the subsequent stability of exchange rates than the sudden, forceful, and concerted intervention that took place in January 1988.

Krugman (1988c) makes a similar point. He uses a simple but elegant model to show how a hard band can modify exchange-rate behaviour even when the market's expectations are based in part on economic fundamentals, rather than irrational moods or fads. If the market believes that the band will be defended firmly, the exchange rate will stay within it despite a change in fundamentals that would have driven a freely floating rate beyond the band. Governments are not relieved of the need to alter their policies when the change in fundamentals appears to be permanent. A long-lasting change in the fundamentals will take the exchange rate to the edge of the band eventually and thus test the governments' credibility. When their commitment is credible, however, there is less volatility within the band and more time to modify policies. There is the obvious risk that time bought will be time wasted, and the slow movement of the rate may even obscure the need for action.[11] But those dangers arise with a soft band too, which allows even more time for procrastination.

Krugman's result helps to explain why pegged exchange rates have tended to remain well within their bands for very long periods, showing very little short-term volatility compared with floating rates. They did this most of the time under the Bretton Woods

System and have continued to do so under the EMS. Some of this short-term stability can be ascribed to intramarginal intervention. But intramarginal intervention has not been frequent enough to explain the whole phenomenon. Most of it must be ascribed to the credibility of the hard band.[12]

Summing up

The rules for exchange-rate management should be as transparent as possible. That is the way to maintain credibility, not by studied ambiguity, which breeds disagreement and distrust.

The need to realign exchange rates periodically argues in favour of wide bands, so that central rates and market rates will not always move together and speculators cannot make one-way bets. But the need to stabilize exchange-rate expectations argues for narrow bands. The conflict between these needs can be resolved in principle by making small realignments very frequently. But that would be difficult politically for the G-7 governments. Therefore, the conflict must be resolved by adopting wider bands than those used in the EMS and relying on the hardness of the bands to stabilize exchange-rate expectations. Hardness is more important than narrowness for this particular purpose.

If governments are not prepared to move in this direction, they may have to retreat from their present stance and be content with episodic exchange-rate management. They cannot expect to manage exchange rates closely and continuously by imprecise, informal understandings, which are bound to produce disagreements among governments as well as misinterpretations by the market. Episodic management can probably flatten exchange-rate movements by bursting speculative bubbles or shaking the market's confidence in its expectations. Experience suggests, however, that decisions to engage in episodic management are taken much too late. When exchange-rate stability disappears from the short list of policy objectives to which governments subscribe continuously, they must agree to reinstate it, and that can be difficult. It took more than three years to persuade the United States that something must be done about the strong dollar. Furthermore, a continuing commitment to exchange-rate stability is likely to be more effective than a sudden flurry of concern in mobilizing domestic political support for the appropriate policy changes.

Capital mobility, crises, and controls

These strong conclusions are based in part on the reading of two stories – the history of successful stabilization in the EMS and the less happy history of stabilization by the G-7 governments. It is therefore necessary to look more closely at the history of the EMS. To what extent has its success been due to special circumstances?

Part of the answer was given in Chapter 3, which identified the circumstances that have made it possible for EMS members to realign exchange rates frequently and speedily, without always waiting for speculative pressures to force their hand. But another question has to be answered. Why have speculative pressures been so small, compared with those that bedevilled the Bretton Woods System? Shouldn't they be much larger now, since capital mobility is much higher?

Under the assumptions usually adopted to model exchange-rate crises, governments that suffer them ought not to complain about them. They richly deserve what they get. In the simplest crisis model,[13] the government adopts a monetary policy that is fundamentally inconsistent with its pegged exchange rate. It creates more money than the public wants to hold and thus starts to lose reserves. The market watches the situation, comparing the government's dwindling reserves with the size of the speculative attack that the market itself will mount as soon as it becomes manifestly clear that the domestic currency would depreciate if the government ceased to defend it. When reserves fall below that critical level, the market pounces, the government loses the rest of its reserves, and the market is vindicated. The domestic currency must be allowed to float and does indeed depreciate. Speculative pressures do not build up gradually. The government is given no warning to change its policies. One day, it has enough reserves to defend the exchange rate for some time to come. The next day, it has none.

In more elaborate models,[14] speculative pressures can build up slowly, because expectations are not unanimous or held with certainty, and the government is given time to reassess its policies. But there is another possibility. The market can misjudge the situation but be completely vindicated because it has made a self-fulfilling prophesy. It can predict and produce the 'collapse' of a pegged exchange rate or, less catastrophically, an exchange-rate realignment, which would not have taken place if the market had not predicted it. Speculative runs on pegged exchange rates can come out of nowhere, just like speculative bubbles under floating rates.

The simple crisis model can tell us what to look for when trying to decide why the EMS has not been plagued by exchange-rate crises. Crises are likely to arise when the market can persuade itself to predict a realignment, when a large amount of capital can be expected to move in response to that prediction, and when the governments' reserves are small compared with the stock of footloose capital.

European governments have tried to discourage the market from predicting realignments. They have stressed the convergence of their monetary policies and sought to reinforce their point by using intramarginal intervention to keep exchange rates from reaching and resting at the edges of their bands:

> On the one hand, the flexibility provided by the fluctuation margins was regarded as a cushion to absorb ... external shocks without the need for immediate changes in basic policies or central rates. Full use of the fluctuation margins would also help to limit exchange market intervention and thus avoid some of its potentially undesirable consequences. On the other hand, there are arguments in favor of keeping the exchange rate stable ... [The] authorities hope to influence market sentiments and exchange rate expectations by showing determination and by preventing the building up of a momentum for exchange rate movements ... [The] latter view has gained favor, and a number of EMS central banks have adopted a strategy of keeping their exchange rates well within the band of the EMS and minimizing movements against key currencies (Ungerer, et al., 1986, p. 5).

This approach, however, has make it harder to keep the market from placing one-way bets when realignments are expected, and the validity of this objection is receiving more attention. It was acknowledged formally in the Basle-Nyborg agreement of 1987, liberalizing EMS credit arrangements.[15]

Limitations on capital mobility have also played a role in combating speculative pressures. France and Italy have used capital controls (and Italy tightened them sharply in 1987 because of speculation against the lira).[16] Belgium has relied on dual exchange rates for current and capital transactions. Belief that these have been important in limiting capital outflows is the source of growing concern about the viability of the EMS as 1992 approaches and capital controls must be dismantled. But another feature of the EMS has probably been more important than capital controls in limiting speculative pressures. The mark is the only world-class currency in the EMS, and it has been the strongest currency for most of the last decade.

Suppose that the foreign-exchange market comes to expect a revaluation of the mark vis-à-vis the French franc. Frenchmen will sell francs for marks. But they are the only large holders of francs. Anyone else wanting to speculate against the franc must borrow francs to sell them. This limits the volume of speculation and turns it around rapidly; Frenchmen need their francs for domestic transactions, and others must repay their debts.[17] Now suppose that Margaret Thatcher changes her mind and Britain becomes a full member of the EMS, bringing in another world-class currency. What will happen when the foreign-exchange market comes to expect a revaluation of the mark vis-à-vis the pound? There are many more footloose holders of sterling than footloose holders of francs, and a much larger amount of capital would move from London to Frankfurt than has typically moved from Paris to Frankfurt. Furthermore, this would not be borrowed money, though that would move too, which means that it might not return rapidly to London.

It is impossible to quantify the importance of this built-in limitation on capital mobility within the EMS. But one point is starkly clear. There is no such limitation on capital mobility in the outside world, among the most important G-7 currencies. Four of them, indeed, are world-class currencies.

But the most important single feature of the EMS has not yet been mentioned. A self-fulfilling speculative crisis cannot take place unless the market can commit larger sums of money than governments can mobilize. The market must be able to swallow their reserves. That cannot happen in the EMS, where governments can mobilize infinite amounts by drawing on reciprocal credit facilities.[18]

Before the Basle-Nyborg agreement of 1987, those facilities were not available for financing intramarginal intervention, and they were not used extensively.[19] But they are there when needed, and the market knows it. That is why the EMS has been more successful than the Bretton Woods System in dealing with speculative pressures.

5

IMPROVING RESERVE ARRANGEMENTS

Extending the agenda

Thus far, we have been concerned with the rationale and methods for managing exchange rates. But these issues open up others. Can the G-7 governments devise reserve arrangements sufficiently elastic to combat speculative pressures? What else should they do to modify reserve arrangements in order to manage exchange rates systematically? How closely must governments coordinate their macroeconomic policies to avoid large and frequent exchange-rate realignments? Have they to coordinate their fiscal policies as well as their monetary policies?

This chapter examines reserve arrangements. It pays particular attention to the asymmetries arising from the central role of the dollar in the international monetary system and the need to augment US reserves if the United States is to participate actively in managing exchange rates. The next chapter examines the problems of policy coordination. It criticizes certain widely held views about the aims of policy coordination, examines the obstacles to closer coordination, and stresses the need for focusing sharply on the compatibility of fiscal policies and integrating the multilateral surveillance of national policies with the domestic policy-making processes of the G-7 governments.

Intervention and reserves

To put hard bands around exchange rates, governments must be prepared to intervene extensively on foreign-exchange markets.

Intervention is always possible for a government that wants to prevent its currency from appreciating; it has merely to purchase foreign currency and pay for it by issuing more of its own currency. If it does not want its money supply to grow, it will try to sterilize its intervention, and this will be difficult when foreign and domestic assets are close substitutes. But problems on this score do not call into question the feasibility of intervention.

Intervention is not always possible for a government that wants to prevent its currency from depreciating; it has to purchase its own currency and pay for it with foreign currency, and it cannot issue foreign currency. It must hold foreign-currency reserves or have reliable access to them. Access can include the right to buy foreign currencies from foreign governments using other acceptable assets such as gold, SDRs, or ECUs, and the right to borrow foreign currencies from governments or international institutions such as the IMF.[1]

The Articles of Agreement of the IMF do not mention currency reserves explicitly. The version that emerged from the Bretton Woods Conference of 1944 reflected the expectation that governments would hold their reserves in gold and that the United States would buy and sell gold for dollars to make them available as needed. The resources of the IMF itself consisted of gold and national currencies deposited by members, and they could draw on those resources to supplement their own reserves. In 1969, the Articles of Agreement were amended to provide for the creation of Special Drawing Rights to supplement supplies of other reserve assets. In 1978, moreover, the next amendment gave the SDR a much bigger role. It was to become 'the principal reserve asset in the international monetary system' (Art. XXII), and all references to gold were expunged (except those restricting the use of gold or relating to the disposition of the Fund's own holdings).

From the earliest years following World War II, however, the dollar has been the principal reserve asset, and that is still true today. Indeed, it continues to be the most important international currency. Its domain has been shrinking slowly, but more slowly than the economic dominance of the United States. Yet the further reform of exchange-rate arrangements may call for significant changes in reserve and reserve-credit arrangements involving a further reduction in the role of the dollar as a reserve asset, which may in turn reduce its relative importance as an international currency.

Changes in reserve arrangements are needed for three purposes. First, the supply of currency reserves must be sufficiently elastic in the short run to combat speculative pressures but sufficiently inelastic in the long run to keep governments from using reserves to finance long-lasting balance-of-payments deficits. The market must know that speculative pressures cannot force governments to realign exchange rates. But governments must know that they cannot postpone adjustment indefinitely – and each government must be confident that its partners know it. Second, reserve arrangements must be made more symmetrical. Present arrangements are asymmetrical in allocating exchange-rate risks and, more fundamentally, in putting appropriate pressures on governments to modify their policies. Finally, the reserves of the United States are far too small, inhibiting its participation in joint intervention and challenging the viability of any commitment it may make to long-lasting exchange-rate management. Its reserves must be enlarged.

The dollar as an international currency
The various tasks of an international currency are listed in Figure 5.1, where they are cross-classified by function and sector.[2] The dollar has done all of them, although its importance has varied from task to task.

The use of the dollar as a unit of account is, perhaps, its least important role. It was never as large in the private sector as casual observers believed, and it has declined in the official sector.

Research on the use of the dollar in international trade was begun by Grassman (1976), who found that the Swedish kronor is the currency most often used to invoice Swedish exports. The dollar came next but far behind. Subsequent research on other industrial countries revealed a similar pattern but assigned even less importance to the dollar. The exporter's currency is used more often than any other to invoice a country's exports, but the importer's currency comes next, ahead of the dollar.[3] In trade with developing countries, by contrast, the dollar is more important than the importing country's currency, and the developing countries' currencies are rarely used to invoice their own exports. In fact, most exports of primary products, including oil, are invoiced in dollars, because they are priced in dollars on international markets.

Figure 5.1 Uses of the dollar as an international currency

Function	Private sector	Official sector
Unit of account	Currency used to invoice trade	Currency used to define central rates
Means of payment	Vehicle currency in foreign-exchange markets	Intervention currency in foreign-exchange markets
Store of value	Currency in which deposits, loans, and bonds are denominated	Currency in which reserves are held

The dollar used to be the principal unit of account in the official sector. Under the Bretton Woods System, most countries pegged their currencies to the dollar and used it to define their central rates. But the pattern is different now. The EMS countries use the ECU to define their central rates, and many developing countries use their own currency 'baskets' or the SDR. In 1974, just after exchange rates began to float, 62 per cent of the developing countries pegged their currencies to the dollar, 24 per cent pegged to other currencies, and 14 per cent did not peg their currencies (Kenen, 1983, Table 13). By 1987, the percentages had changed markedly:[4]

Pegged to the dollar	30
Pegged to other currencies	15
Pegged to the SDR	6
Pegged to other currency baskets	16
Other exchange-rate arrangements	33

The decline in this particular use of the dollar, however, is due directly to the change in exchange-rate arrangements, not the increasing attractiveness of other currencies.

The dollar is far more important as a means of payment in the foreign-exchange market. It is indeed the dominant currency in foreign-exchange trading. In London, for example, 30 per cent of all foreign-exchange transactions involve dollar purchases or sales of sterling, 67 per cent involve dollar purchases or sales of marks, yen, and other currencies, and only 3 per cent involve other pairs of currencies (e.g., sterling purchases or sales of marks or yen). Similar patterns obtain in New York and Tokyo.[5] It is hard to obtain quantitative evidence on the use of the dollar for official intervention, but anecdotal evidence suggests that it is still dominant in this respect too, because it is the vehicle for foreign-exchange trading.[6] There is only one important exception. The EMS countries use EMS currencies for mandatory intervention and for some intramarginal intervention as well. Gross intervention by EMS countries amounted to $477 billion from the founding of the EMS through June 1987. Dollar intervention accounted for 52 per cent, mandatory intervention in EMS currencies for 12 per cent, and intramarginal intervention in EMS currencies for 36 per cent.[7] The figure for dollar intervention includes both intervention designed primarily to affect the value of the dollar (e.g., intervention under the Plaza and Louvre agreements) and intramarginal intervention to affect EMS exchange rates.

The largest changes in the use of the dollar have occurred in its role as a store of value. The trend on the private side is illustrated by developments in the Eurocurrency and Eurobond markets. The trend on the official side is illustrated by the changing composition of currency reserves.

In 1986, about 65 per cent of banks' foreign-currency claims on non-residents were denominated in US dollars, compared with averages of 69 per cent in 1976–80 and 73 per cent in 1971–5. The dollar is still the most important currency in Eurocurrency markets but less important than it was a decade ago.[8] In 1984–6, $493 billion of new bonds and other instruments were issued on international markets, of which $106 billion were issued by US institutions. Dollar issues accounted for 58 per cent of the total and for 54 per cent when US issues are excluded. In 1979–81, when new issues totalled $64 billion, dollar issues accounted for fully 70 per cent of the total and for 64 per cent when US issues are excluded.[9] The share of the dollar has fallen in these markets too.

The dollar was the dominant reserve currency for many years. In 1976, it accounted for almost 80 per cent of total foreign-currency reserves (see Table 5.1). At about that time, however, central banks and governments began to diversify. The developing countries moved first and faster; their dollar holdings amounted to 73 per cent of their currency reserves in 1976, fell to 57 per cent by 1980, and rose a bit thereafter, reaching 60 per cent in 1986. The developed countries started later and moved more slowly; their holdings amounted to 87 per cent of their currency reserves in 1976, fell to 81 per cent in 1980, and continued to fall thereafter, reaching 76 per cent in 1986. (These figures are adjusted to exclude US reserves, which cannot be held in dollars, and do not correspond precisely to those in Table 5.1.)

Table 5.1 National currencies held in official reserves (per cent of total foreign-currency holdings at end of year)

Currency	1976	1978	1980	1982	1984	1986
US dollar	79.6	76.0	67.3	70.7	69.5	66.6
German mark	7.0	10.9	15.2	12.7	12.6	14.8
Japanese yen	0.7	3.3	4.4	4.7	5.7	6.9
Pound sterling	2.0	1.7	3.0	2.5	3.0	2.4
Swiss franc	1.4	2.1	3.2	2.8	2.1	1.6
Other and unspecified	9.3	6.0	6.9	6.6	7.2	7.8

Source: International Monetary Fund, *Annual Report* (various years). Total and dollar reserves include the dollar equivalents of the European Currency Units (ECU) issued against dollars (ECU issued against gold are excluded completely).

Some of the fluctuations shown in Table 5.1 reflect the effects of exchange-rate changes rather than changes in holdings. In 1986, for example, the depreciation of the dollar just about cancelled the increase in the volume of dollar holdings, and the share of the dollar dropped slightly as holdings of other currencies rose. But the longer-term trend is unmistakable evidence of gradual diversification.

The more rapid diversification by developing countries reflects a basic difference between them and the major industrial countries. Small countries can diversify more or less freely, just like private institutions, and one would expect their behaviour to reflect the variables that usually influence portfolio selection (although the use of standard portfolio models to simulate their asset choices have not been very successful). The major industrial countries are constrained in two important ways. First, they cannot hold their own currencies as reserve assets. Japan cannot hold yen; the United States cannot hold dollars. Second, they are constrained by their exchange-rate policies and those of their partners. Japan acquires dollars when it intervenes to keep the dollar from depreciating against the yen. It cannot swap them for marks, however, without making it harder for Germany to keep the dollar from depreciating against the mark.

If allowed to continue for another decade, the diversification of currency reserves will probably produce a multiple reserve-currency system of the sort that some observers have favoured for some time. They believe that it would reduce the influence of US policies on the behaviour of the world economy and limit the ability of the United States to exploit the reserve-currency role of the dollar. Both objectives may have merit but cannot be achieved by moving to a multiple reserve-currency system.

Reducing the role of the dollar as a reserve currency would not necessarily reduce its role in international financial markets, and the latter may be far more important in giving US policies a disproportionate influence on the world economy. Furthermore, the ability of the United States to exploit its role as a reserve-currency country does not depend primarily on the share of the dollar in total currency reserves. It depends on the role of the United States in exchange-rate management. Unless that role is modified, along lines proposed later in this chapter, a further reduction in the share of the dollar as a reserve currency will merely concentrate the consequences of US behaviour on the other G-7 countries. If central banks dissatisfied with US behaviour begin to shift from dollars to yen and the Japanese authorities try to prevent the dollar from depreciating, the Japanese must take up the dollars that others want to shed. These switches, moreover, are most likely to occur precisely when the G-7 governments are called upon to cope with speculative pressures from the private sector.

A multiple reserve-currency system will amplify exchange-rate instability and complicate the task of exchange-rate management unless there are restrictions on the governments' freedom to shift from currency to currency.

Asymmetries and tensions

It is not hard to explain why the dollar became the main international currency after World War II, without even invoking the size of the US economy. It was the only transferable currency in the early postwar years and thus the only available vehicle for foreign-exchange trading, which made it in turn the most convenient intervention currency. Furthermore, US financial markets were not fenced off by capital controls, so foreigners could lend and borrow freely. Therefore, the dollar was an attractive reserve asset for official institutions and a convenient store of value for other foreign asset holders. To which one must add, of course, the convertibility of the dollar into gold for foreign official holders and the strength of the dollar in terms of other currencies, backed by comparative price stability in the United States.

It is equally easy to explain why the various roles of the dollar have contracted unevenly. The convenience of using a vehicle currency in foreign-exchange trading explains why the market will choose only one, and why an established currency does not give way gradually to others.[10] Therefore, the dollar continues to be the vehicle currency and the most important intervention currency although it has ceased to be equally important as an international unit of account or store of value. Furthermore, constraints on diversification have sustained the role of the dollar as a reserve currency. The major industrial countries cannot diversify freely because of their involvement in managing exchange rates.[11]

The uneven decline in the use of the dollar has intensified tensions arising from basic asymmetries produced by two features of the monetary system.

The first is a manifestation of the *N*th country problem. Because there is only one exchange rate linking two national currencies, it is always feasible and may be convenient for one of the two governments to refrain from intervening and leave that task entirely to the other. Joint intervention is not necessary technically, even though it may be more effective tactically. Under the Bretton Woods System, then, the United States left to other governments most of the intervention required to stabilize the dollar. It was passive not only in respect of exchange-rate policy but also in respect of intervention.[12] Therefore, it did not hold large currency reserves but borrowed foreign currencies whenever it chose to intervene for tactical purposes. It drew on bilateral credit lines with foreign central banks and, on one occasion, issued foreign-currency bonds to German investors (the so-called Carter bonds of 1978).

The United States has intervened more actively in the past few years. It bought foreign currencies in 1980 and 1981 to slow down the appreciation of the dollar, and it did so again in 1985 as part of the joint effort by the G-7 governments to drive down the dollar after the Plaza Communiqué. Its foreign-currency reserves rose from

$3.8 billion at the end of 1979 to $17.3 billion at the end of 1986. In 1987 and 1988, moreover, the United States sold foreign currencies to arrest the depreciation of the dollar. From November 1987 through January 1988, for example, it sold $4.1 billion worth of marks and yen, and its foreign-currency reserves had fallen to $11.8 billion at the end of February 1988. But the other G-7 governments have intervened much more heavily. Germany and Japan held $61.3 billion of foreign currencies (mainly dollars) at the end of 1985; their holdings rose to $83.5 billion at the end of 1986 and to $145.9 billion at the end of February 1988.[13]

The second feature of the monetary system that contributes to asymmetry relates to the different effects of intervention on national money supplies. When the Bundesbank intervenes to support the dollar against the mark, it adds dollars to its assets and issues additional marks to pay for them. It must then act deliberately to sterilize its intervention; it must sell off other assets to withdraw the marks. But German intervention does not affect the US money supply, because the Bundesbank invests its dollars in US government securities rather than holding them with the Federal Reserve Bank of New York. In other words, the effects of German intervention on the US money supply are sterilized automatically and pose no challenge to the conduct of US monetary policy.*

A similar asymmetry can sometimes develop when the United States intervenes, because US reserves are held partly by the Treasury, not the Federal Reserve, and some of them are held at foreign central banks, not in government securities. When the US Treasury sells marks for dollars in order to support the dollar, it uses the dollars to retire debt. There is no change in the US money supply.[14] But the marks it sells to buy the dollars may be transferred on the books of the Bundesbank, from the account of the US Treasury to those of German commercial banks that held the dollars initially. This amounts to issuing new money in Germany. Therefore, the Bundesbank must act deliberately to sterilize the effects of

---

*If the Bundesbank held its dollars with the New York Federal Reserve Bank, it would have them transferred from the commercial bank where they resided when it bought them, and this would reduce the US money supply. To sterilize the effects of German intervention, the Federal Reserve would have to make an open-market purchase of US government securities. By investing its newly acquired dollars in US government securities, the Bundesbank compresses this process, but the securities end up with the Bundesbank, not with the Federal Reserve.

US intervention on the German money supply, just as it must act deliberately to sterilize the effects of its own intervention.*

These institutional features of the system result in two asymmetries when intervention is required to support the dollar. First, the United States does not bear much of the exchange-rate risk. Germany, Japan, and other countries increase their dollar holdings by more than the United States reduces its foreign-currency holdings or adds to its foreign-currency debt. In effect, the United States is able to borrow in its own currency. Second, other countries face an increase in their money supplies that has to be offset deliberately and cannot always be offset fully.[15] But there is no such problem for the United States, where the money supply does not fall because it is insulated automatically from other countries' purchases of dollars. Monetary growth can continue in the United States, and the balance-of-payments adjustment process develops an inflationary bias.

The problem can be put more generally. When other governments acquire dollars and cannot convert them into other reserve assets, the United States does not lose reserves. This is the 'exorbitant privilege' to which President de Gaulle objected many years ago, and others have also objected to it. In the 1960s, American multinationals were accused of 'buying up' Europe with dollars lent back to the United States by foreign governments, and the Pentagon was accused of using those dollars to finance the Vietnam war. These are simplistic accusations but not utter nonsense. The reserve-currency role of the dollar has allowed the United States more freedom to pursue its economic and political objectives. In the 1980s, moreover, the problem took a new form. Foreign governments objected strongly to the US budget deficit but were obliged to finance and monetize part of it. In 1986 and 1987, foreign official purchases of US government securities were bigger than those of the Federal Reserve System.

The Plaza and Louvre agreements have made the monetary system somewhat more symmetrical. The United States has been involved more actively in intervention. But it has done much less than others, partly because it has rather small reserves. At

---

*The mechanics are more complicated when US intervention is conducted by the Federal Reserve or financed by drawings on central-bank credit lines. The foreign effects are the same as those described in the text, but the domestic effects are not. The dollars bought by the Federal Reserve are withdrawn from the US money supply, and the domestic effects of US intervention are not sterilized automatically.

the end of 1987, it held less than $35 billion in foreign currencies and readily usable claims on the IMF, a sum only half as large as German and Japanese *purchases* of dollars in 1987. But there are ways of raising more.

In the 1960s, the United States set up bilateral credit arrangements with foreign central banks, and they have been enlarged.[16] The swap lines with other G-7 countries currently total $21 billion, and those with Switzerland and the Bank for International Settlements (BIS) bring the total close to $27 billion. Furthermore, the US quota in the IMF is nearly $20 billion, and it can draw about $5 billion almost automatically. Finally, the United States holds 262 million ounces of gold, which it values at $11 billion. At current market prices, however, it is worth about $118 billion. If the United States tried to sell its gold, it would drive the price down sharply. But there are ways to turn some gold into other, more usable, reserve assets at a price related to the current market price.

Renovation rather than reform

Let us return to the issues raised at the beginning of this chapter. How can reserve arrangements be made more symmetrical and sufficiently elastic in the short run to ward off speculative pressures?

It is tempting to draw up another ambitious plan for reforming the whole monetary system – to make the SDR 'the principal reserve asset' and give the IMF a larger role in managing the system. But I have done that before,[17] and this is not the time for launching such a plan. European governments are more interested in the evolution of the EMS and in the ECU than the SDR. The United States should be more interested in the exchange-rate regime and in modest modifications of reserve arrangements to help it participate more fully in exchange-rate management.

Comprehensive reform, moreover, would require another amendment to the Articles of Agreement of the IMF, and that would require the consent of developing countries. But they would want to deal with other issues as well: the conditionality of access to IMF facilities and a long-term solution to their own debt problem. These issues have to be addressed, more urgently perhaps than those considered here, but this is an instance in which it may be unwise to put too many issues on a single bargaining table.

Two steps can be taken quickly, however, without amending the

Articles of Agreement. (1) Reserve supplies can be made more elastic in the short run by altering the terms of the existing swap arrangements and adopting additional guidelines or rules for funding them over the long term. (2) Exchange-rate risks can be redistributed and US reserves increased by reviving and extending a proposal made some years ago to establish a 'substitution account' under IMF auspices.[18]

Credit facilities and foreign-currency borrowing

The bilateral swap arrangements are similar in many ways to the very short-term credit facilities of the EMS, but there are two important differences. The EMS facilities are fully automatic and are open-ended for purposes of mandatory intervention.[19] Furthermore, drawings on the EMS facilities can be rolled over automatically within certain limits, and they can be funded partially by using the longer-term credit facilities of the European Monetary Cooperation Fund (EMCF). Funding is not always necessary because speculative capital movements tend to reverse themselves, and it is not available unconditionally. The EMS facilities are very elastic in the short run but less elastic in the long run. The G-7 governments may not be ready to follow these precedents completely – to make the bilateral swap arrangements open-ended and fully automatic. But doubling or tripling the present limits would have much the same effect. This enlargement, however, would have to be accompanied by a more liberal agreement on funding. Otherwise, governments will hesitate to use the swaps more freely.

There are three ways in which a government can repay short-term foreign-currency debt. It can draw on its foreign-currency reserves and SDR holdings. It can draw on its IMF quota. It can fund its short-term debt by issuing long-term debt to its creditors or directly to the public at large. The United States cannot make much use of the first and second methods. Its reserves are too small, and it cannot draw heavily on its IMF quota without obvious political embarrassment – which might give some joy to those who have gone through it but would probably discourage the United States from drawing on the swap lines. But it can issue foreign-currency bonds. It issued the so-called Roosa bonds to foreign governments in the early 1960s and sold the so-called Carter bonds directly to German investors in 1978.

The United States has been urged repeatedly to issue foreign-currency debt as a way of reviving capital inflows and thus covering its trade and budget deficits. Foreign investors, it is said, are reluctant to buy more dollar-denominated bonds but would be eager to buy US government securities denominated in marks and yen. Furthermore, the offer would be taken as a promise by the US government to defend the dollar by making the necessary policy changes, because a further depreciation would raise the cost of servicing the debt.[20]

Some of the enthusiasm for this proposal appears to reflect the markets' love of dealing in new instruments and deriving a menagerie of other instruments from them – a whole new zoo of yencats and other animals. The proposal has also met with strong objections – one symbolic and the other substantive. The US government owes much more to foreigners than does Brazil or Mexico, but it has been able to borrow in its own currency. Having to borrow in foreign currency might be more embarrassing than having to draw heavily on the IMF. Furthermore, US government bonds issued in marks or yen might be more attractive to American investors than to Germans or Japanese, and it would be difficult to turn them away. Bonds sold to Americans, moreover, would not help to cover the trade deficit because they would not generate a capital inflow. The Carter bonds of 1978 were sold only to German investors, and the German authorities helped to enforce that limitation. But the amounts involved were comparatively small.[21]

This last objection suggests that foreign-currency bonds should not be used to fund short-term debt when the dollar is weak. If they attracted American investors, the US Treasury would have to sell large quantities in order to repay small amounts of short-term debt. They can serve that purpose most efficiently only after speculative pressures have subsided. But this limitation would not impair their usefulness if suitable guidelines were adopted, permitting a debtor government to roll over short-term debt or to issue long-term debt to creditor governments until the time is ripe for marketing debt directly to the public. Such guidelines should also permit a debtor to issue long-term debt to a creditor government if that government objects to the marketing of debt in its domestic capital market, fearing that it might 'crowd out' the creditor's own borrowing. But creditor governments can be expected to favour the marketing of long-term debt directly to the public; it would serve to sterilize the money-supply effects of the intervention financed initially by drawings on short-term credit lines.

A substitution account

A substitution account could make the monetary system more symmetrical by raising the readily usable reserves of the United States and reducing the exchange-rate risks already borne by other countries. How would it work?

Under arrangements proposed in 1979, when the subject was under discussion in the IMF, governments and central banks holding dollar balances would have deposited some of those balances with the IMF in exchange for an SDR-denominated claim. The claims could not have been used directly for intervention, because the foreign-exchange market does not deal in SDRs, but could have been sold to other participating governments in exchange for those governments' currencies. It was agreed in principle that the depositors would share with the United States the costs and benefits of the arrangement. Washington interpreted this to mean that the United States and the depositors would share any losses incurred by the account when and if the account was liquidated. Such losses would occur if the dollar had depreciated vis-à-vis the SDR in the intervening years.

The discussions broke down in 1980, however, when potential depositors rejected the American interpretation and the United States shifted its own position, proposing that any and all losses be borne by the IMF itself, which would set aside some of its gold for that purpose. In fact, the whole proposal became less attractive as the dollar began to appreciate.[22] I am fond of quoting the US official who was heard to complain that there is never a good time for reforming the monetary system. When the dollar is weak, the United States cannot exercise leadership; when the dollar is strong, no one else is interested.

The 1979 proposal would have reduced the exchange-rate risks borne by dollar holders but would not have enlarged US reserves. A variant on that proposal would do both, and also cover losses that might have to be met if and when the account is liquidated. The United States would deposit gold. Other governments would deposit dollars. Both would obtain an SDR-denominated claim to be used as a reserve asset. A numerical example will help here.

Figure 5.2 The balance sheet of the substitution account (in billions of SDR unless otherwise indicated)

A. Initial situation:

Assets		Liabilities and capital	
Gold at 95 per cent of market price: 90 million ounces	28.5	SDR claims of participants: United States	21.0
Dollar deposits at SDR price:		Other governments	60.0
$81 billion	60.0	Capital	7.5
Total	88.5	Total	88.5

Accounting prices:
Dollar price of the SDR .... 1.35 dollars per SDR
Dollar price of gold .... 450.00 dollars per ounce
SDR price of gold .... 333.33 SDRs per ounce

B. After dollar depreciation but with constant dollar gold price:

Assets		Liabilities and capital	
Gold at 95 per cent of market price: 90 million ounces	26.1	SDR claims of participants: United States	21.0
Dollar deposits at SDR price:		Other governments	60.0
$81 billion	54.9	Capital	—
Total	81.0	Total	81.0

Accounting prices:
Dollar price of the SDR .... 1.475 dollars per SDR
Dollar price of gold .... Unchanged
SDR price of gold .... 305.508 SDRs per ounce

C. After dollar depreciation but with constant SDR gold price:

Assets		Liabilities and capital	
Gold at 95 per cent of market price: 90 million ounces	28.5	SDR claims of participants: United States	21.0
Dollar deposits at SDR price:		Other governments	60.0
$81 billion	52.5	Capital	—
Total	81.0	Total	81.0

Accounting prices:
Dollar price of the SDR .... 1.543 dollars per SDR
Dollar price of gold .... 514.286 dollars per ounce
SDR price of gold .... Unchanged

Suppose that the account had been opened early in 1988, when the SDR was valued at about $1.35 and the market price of gold was about $450 per ounce. Suppose that the United States had deposited 90 million ounces of gold, about a third of its total holdings, and that the gold was valued for this purpose at 70 per cent of its market price. The United States would have been credited with 21 billion of SDR claims. The account, however, might have carried the gold at 95 per cent of its market value, the equivalent of 28.5 billion SDRs. Suppose that other governments had deposited $81 billion of dollar balances, slightly more than 30 per cent of their holdings in the United States. They would have been credited with 60 billion of SDR claims.

The initial balance sheet of the account is shown at (A) in Figure 5.2. Its assets would have been worth 88.5 billion SDRs; its obligations to the participating countries would have amounted to 81.0 billion; and it would have had capital worth 7.5 billion – a reserve against possible losses resulting from exchange-rate changes and changes in the price of gold.

Now look ahead to the time at which the account is liquidated. How far can the dollar fall before the capital is wiped out, forcing the United States and other participants to share the losses of the account? Much depends on the behaviour of the gold price.

If the price of gold remained constant in dollars, the dollar value of the SDR would have to rise from $1.35 to $1.475 per SDR to wipe out the capital of the account. In other words, the dollar would have to depreciate by more than 9 per cent against the SDR and by nearly 14 per cent against the other currencies that make up the SDR.[23] This result is shown at (B) in Figure 5.2. If the price of gold remained constant in SDRs, however, the dollar value of the SDR would have to rise to $1.543 per SDR to wipe out the capital of the account. The dollar would have to depreciate by more than 14 per cent against the SDR and by more than 21 per cent against the other currencies. This is the result shown at (C) in Figure 5.2. It should be emphasized, moreover, that these calculations pertain to a rather remote contingency – the total liquidation of the account (although large losses early on might have to be made up provisionally by depositing additional gold or dollars).

Many difficult problems would have to be solved before the account could be created – problems pertaining to the transferability of the SDR claim, its relationship to the 'ordinary' SDR issued by the IMF, and the interest rates payable to the account and to the depositors. But all of these issues were discussed exhaustively a few years ago and did not produce deep disagreements. Those arose mainly with regard to the problem of solvency, examined above, and deposits of gold by the United States would help to solve that problem. Furthermore, the United States would benefit directly, because it could exchange some of its gold holdings for a readily usable reserve asset.

If the United States could obtain an additional $21 billion of SDR claims in this manner and the existing swap lines were doubled, it would have or could borrow usable assets totalling more than $120 billion. They would be nearly twice as large as in 1987.[24] It would not be possible for the United States to use all of them simultaneously, and that would not be prudent in any case. It should draw on them sequentially, using its SDR claims to repay drawings on the swap lines when it was not possible to repay them by selling foreign-currency debt directly to private investors. Nevertheless, the numbers are impressive. They should dispel any doubt about the ability of the United States to participate fully in exchange-rate management by taking on a larger share of the required intervention.

6

COORDINATING NATIONAL POLICIES

Perspectives on policy coordination

Governments engage in many forms of economic cooperation. They exchange information about their economies, forecasts, and policies. They provide financial assistance to other governments, bilaterally and multilaterally, ranging from balance-of-payments support to long-term development assistance. They act jointly to supervise or regulate various sorts of economic activity. Policy coordination is the most rigorous form of cooperation. It involves mutually agreed modifications in the participants' national policies. In the macroeconomic domain, it involves explicit commitments about the conduct of monetary and fiscal policies. The agreement may be framed in terms of the governments' policy targets – growth rates, inflation rates, and so on – but must also identify the policy instruments that governments will use to pursue them.[1]

Policy coordination can result from *ad hoc* bargaining about particular targets and instruments or from an agreement to follow certain rules or guidelines. The Bonn Summit of 1978 is usually cited as the leading instance of *ad hoc* bargaining, although the bargain was not confined to macroeconomic matters. Germany and Japan made promises about their fiscal policies, and the United States made promises about its energy policies.[2] The 1944 agreement to establish the Bretton Woods System is sometimes cited as a bargain about rules, because governments undertook to change their domestic policies when those policies came into conflict with their exchange-rate obligations.

Some would say that those undertakings were too vague to qualify as rules and that they were not mutual. Deficit countries had to modify their policies but surplus countries did not, and the same complaint is made about the EMS. But mutuality and symmetry are not the same. The Bretton Woods System was not symmetrical, although the most striking asymmetries were those that exempted the United States from the obligations borne by other deficit countries, rather than those that distinguished deficit from surplus countries. Nevertheless, the undertakings were mutual in an important contingent sense. They applied in principle to every country when it ran a balance-of-payments deficit.

The Louvre Accord of 1987 can be described as a combination of the two techniques for policy coordination. There were rule-based obligations, loosely defined perhaps, which linked the use of interest-rate policies to the maintenance of exchange-rate stability. There was an *ad hoc* bargain about fiscal policies, although it served mainly to codify goals that the governments had already chosen unilaterally.

Another distinction proves to be useful in analysing policy coordination and the various obstacles to it. Coordination may be viewed as the logical extension of an optimizing process by which governments pursue their policy objectives. Most economists have adopted this perspective to model and measure the gains from coordination. It can be described for convenience as the policy-optimizing approach to coordination. Valuable insights can be gained, however, when policy coordination is viewed as the process by which governments pursue commonly agreed or collective objectives. This can be described for convenience as the regime-preserving or public-goods approach to coordination.[3]

Many economists find it useful to portray policy formation as an optimizing process. Each government is deemed to have a welfare function defined in terms of policy targets such as real growth and price stability. It sets out to maximize that function by choosing the most appropriate combination of policy instruments – interest rates, tax rates, and so on.

Suppose that each government acts independently. Its decisions may affect other governments' decisions, but it disregards that possibility. When governments behave this way, they will wind up in a suboptimal situation, known as the non-cooperative or Nash equilibrium. They have neglected the policy interdependence resulting from structural interdependence. Japan will not necessarily change its policies just because it has observed a change in US policies. It is bound to change them eventually, however, when the new US policies begin to affect the Japanese economy. But governments can bargain their way to a better situation, known as the cooperative or Pareto equilibrium. By changing the settings of their policy instruments in a mutually agreed manner, each government can get closer to its own national targets and thus raise the value of its welfare function.[4]

Viewed from this standpoint, policy coordination serves to internalize the effects of economic interdependence that no single government can capture on its own by setting its policies unilaterally. To use a different metaphor, policy coordination gives each government partial control over other governments' policy instruments. Therefore, it relieves the shortage of instruments that prevents each government from reaching its own targets.[5]

Some economists, political scientists, and policy-makers take a different view of policy coordination.[6] It is needed to produce certain public goods and defend the international economic system from economic and political shocks, including misbehaviour by governments themselves.

Much of this important work was performed by the United States in the early postwar decades. It was the hegemonic power, with the ability and self-interested concern to stabilize the world economy by its own efforts. Furthermore, it had been largely responsible for writing the rules of the system and designing the institutions, and it could be expected to defend them whenever they were threatened. Equally important, other governments could not accomplish very much without American cooperation. Matters are different today. It is still difficult to do very much without American cooperation, and little is likely to happen until Washington decides that something must be done. But the United States cannot act alone. The economic and political costs are too high.

It is easy to find instances of regime-preserving cooperation in recent economic history. They include the mobilization of financial support for the dollar and sterling in the 1960s and the joint operation of the London gold pool, the 'rescue' of the dollar in 1978, the speedy provision of bridge loans to Mexico at the start of the debt crisis in 1982, and the Plaza Communiqué of 1985, which was meant to defend the trade regime rather than alter the exchange-rate regime.

The bargain struck at Bonn in 1978 can also be described as regime-preserving coordination. It reflected an agreed need for collective action on two fronts: for more vigorous recovery from the global recession of 1974–5, to combat rising unemployment, especially in Europe, and for energy conservation to reduce the industrial countries' dependence on imported oil and limit the ability of OPEC to raise oil prices.

When viewed from this different perspective, policy coordination becomes the logical response to the dispersion of power and influence that ended American hegemony. Public goods must be produced and institutional arrangements defended by joint action. When seen this way, moreover, disagreements about the benefits and costs of policy coordination take on a different but familiar aspect. They become debates about burden-sharing.

Two views of exchange-rate management
The two views of policy coordination give us different ways of looking at exchange-rate management. Seen from the policy-optimizing viewpoint, it is the use of a policy rule to internalize the effects of economic interdependence, a workable compromise between fully optimal coordination and the neglect of interdependence. Seen from the regime-preserving viewpoint, it embodies a commitment by governments to pursue exchange-rate stability as a public good – an objective in its own right.[7]

The earliest theoretical work on policy-optimizing coordination dealt mainly with the pegged-rate case. Recent work has taken the opposite tack, because of the change in the actual exchange-rate regime and because mathematical tractability exerts an enormous influence on the economist's research agenda.

Many economists doubt that exchange-rate expectations are truly rational, yet they tend to disparage or dismiss any other view. But it is hard to solve a theoretical model in which rational expectations are combined with imperfect capital mobility. Accordingly, most such models assume that foreign and domestic assets are perfect substitutes. On this assumption, however, exchange-rate pegging precludes any other use of monetary policy, limiting the scope for policy coordination. Therefore, exchange-rate pegging is typically seen as an alternative to discretionary coordination. It is attractive mainly because a rule-based regime is less vulnerable to cheating or reneging, which economists have regarded as a major obstacle to fully optimal coordination.[8]

The regime-preserving view invites a more generous interpretation of exchange-rate pegging. It can be the most attractive framework for policy coordination when governments attach enough importance to exchange-rate stability as a public good. The key questions pertain to the costs of producing it. On this view, of course, the Louvre Accord represents another instance of regime-preserving coordination. It began as an effort to keep the dollar from 'overshooting' and allow the adjustment process to work itself out, but became more ambitious as the G-7 governments started to pursue exchange-rate stability as an objective in its own right.

The obstacles to policy coordination
Economists have used the policy-optimizing framework to measure the potential gains from coordination. An early attempt by Oudiz and Sachs (1984) found that they were disappointingly small. In one of their exercises, for example, coordination of fiscal and monetary policies by Germany, Japan, and the United States had very little influence on the fiscal instruments and rather small effects on economic performance. When measured in units equivalent to percentage-point changes in real income, the welfare gains were smaller than one per cent of GNP. But subsequent studies have produced bigger numbers. Holtham and Hughes Hallett (1987) have reported welfare gains, measured in income-equivalent units, as large as 6 or 7 per cent of GNP and no smaller than 3 or 4 per cent, depending on the model used. There would thus seem to be unexploited gains from policy-optimizing coordination.

Why don't governments exploit these gains? Four reasons are frequently given.[9] First, governments are apt to renege on their bargains and cannot trust each other. Second, governments subscribe to different views about economic behaviour and the workings of the world economy. Third, governments have different policy targets. Fourth, political and constitutional constraints interfere with the bargaining process.

The first explanation has been thoroughly demolished. The rest make sense. But they seem more cogent when they are invoked to explain the apparent scarcity of regime-preserving coordination than when they are used to account for a shortage of policy-optimizing coordination.

The concern about reneging derives in large part from the stylized way in which many economists have represented public and private decision-making. Recall the example given in Chapter 4, where the government announced its monetary policy and the private sector made binding wage and price decisions in light of its forecast for inflation, which was based on its expectation about monetary policy. A short-sighted government would be tempted to cheat – to follow a monetary policy different from the one it had announced, so as to raise output and employment by exploiting the short-run fixity of wages and prices. But a far-sighted government is apt to resist that temptation in order to protect its reputation, and its resistance is increased when it is involved simultaneously in many sequential games – some with its own citizens and some with foreign governments.

Governments try to avoid making commitments that they cannot expect to honour and try to honour those they make:

If we take seriously the claim that policy-makers in an anarchic world are constantly tempted to cheat, certain features of the [1978] Bonn story – certain things that did *not* happen – seem quite anomalous. We find little evidence that the negotiations were hampered by mutual fear of reneging. For example, even though the Bonn agreement was negotiated with exquisite care, it contained no special provisions about phasing or partial conditionality that might have protected the parties from unexpected defection. Moreover, the Germans and the Japanese both irretrievably enacted their parts of the bargain in September, more than six months before [President Carter's] action on oil price decontrol and nearly two years before decontrol was implemented.

Once the Germans and Japanese had fulfilled their parts of the bargain, the temptation to the President to renege should have been overpowering, if the standard account of international anarchy is to be believed. Moreover, the domestic political pressure on him to renege was clearly very strong. But virtually no one on either side of the final decontrol debate dismissed the Bonn pledge as irrelevant (Putnam and Henning, 1986, p. 100).

But these results should not surprise us when we treat the Bonn bargain as an exercise in regime-preserving coordination and bear in mind the complex and continuing relationships among the participants. Each government stood to gain from its own 'concessions' as well as from those of its partners, and each was concerned to preserve its reputation for reliability. In President Carter's own words, 'Each of us has been careful not to promise more than he can deliver.'[10]

Governments *do* disagree about economic behaviour. German and American governments have disagreed for years about the responsiveness of unemployment to aggregate demand, and even about the way that aggregate demand responds to fiscal and monetary policies. For a time, moreover, US officials denied that there was any connection between the American budget and trade deficits, while other governments connected them simplistically, without leaving enough room for the role of the exchange rate.[11] But economists disagree in turn about the way in which disagreements among governments affect policy coordination.

Frankel and Rockett (1988) have tried to show that misperceptions about economic behaviour can lead to welfare-worsening policy bargains. They use ten large multi-country models to represent US and European views about economic behaviour and assume that each party uses its own model to measure the welfare effects of striking a bargain with the other. The governments do not exchange information; instead, they agree to coordinate their policies whenever each government's calculations lead it to believe that coordination will be beneficial, given its own model and policy targets.

After they have taken the governments through the bargaining process and know the new settings of the policy instruments, Frankel and Rockett ask what will happen to the world economy, using the 'true' economic model. Because they must measure the effects of every bargain using all ten models, they must analyse 100 potential bargains and 1,000 possible outcomes. They find that the United States gains in 494 cases, loses in 398, and is unaffected in the remaining 108, while Europe gains in 477 cases, loses in 418, and is unaffected in the remaining 105. Both parties' 'failure rates' are about 40 per cent.

These are interesting results, but they must be interpreted cautiously. Frankel himself concludes that 'ministers in G-5 and Summit Meetings might do better to discuss their beliefs directly, rather than simply telling each other how they should adjust their policies' (Frankel, 1987b, p. 31). But that is what governments have been doing all along, and there is a simple way to represent the outcome.

Suppose as before that each government adheres to one model and also knows the other's model. If it is not perfectly confident about the rightness of its views, prudential considerations should lead it to ask how a policy bargain would affect its welfare on the working supposition that the other government is using the right model; it should not strike a bargain unless it can expect to gain under both governments' models. If it wants to persuade its partner to accept its own proposals – an important part of the actual bargaining process – reputational considerations should lead it to make sure that its own proposals would raise its partner's welfare under both governments' models. These concerns, taken together, impose a strong condition on the bargaining process: it should not even start unless both governments can expect to gain under both governments' models.

Holtham and Hughes Hallett (1987) came to this conclusion by a different route and applied this strong condition to the Frankel-Rockett bargains. They used six models, not ten, and had thus to analyse 36 possible bargains. But they ruled out 20 of these bargains, because they violated the strong condition.[12] This leads to the first conclusion: disagreements about economic behaviour can be a major obstacle to policy-optimizing coordination. They can keep governments from getting together. But Holtham and Hughes Hallett went on to measure the welfare effects of the other 16 bargains, and they found that the failure rate was quite low. It was 27 per cent for the United States and 17 per cent for Europe.[13] This leads to the second conclusion: when prudential and reputational considerations block bargains that should not take place, policy coordination is not very dangerous to the participants' health.

No one has made similar calculations for an instance of regime-preserving coordination. But one would expect similar results. When governments disagree about the workings of the world economy, they are bound to hold different views about the costs of policy coordination and their distribution, even when they agree completely about the benefits. Suppose that two governments are considering the use of interest-rate policies for exchange-rate stabilization. If they hold different views about the effects of interest rates on aggregate demand, they will disagree about the costs of exchange-rate stabilization.

Disagreements about economic behaviour may be particularly potent in blocking this sort of coordination. When governments are willing to contemplate policy-optimizing coordination, it must be because they believe that they can make welfare-improving changes in their own national policies if their partners do so too. When governments are made to contemplate regime-preserving coordination, they may still believe that their policies are optimal and will be reluctant to modify their policies.

The same possibility arises when governments have different policy objectives – the third in the list of reasons for the apparent scarcity of coordination. In fact, such differences cannot explain why governments fail to engage in policy-optimizing coordination. On the contrary, they make it more attractive.

An example drawn from Eichengreen (1985) illustrates this point. Indeed, it makes a stronger point. Governments that have incompatible objectives can nevertheless benefit from policy coordination.

Consider two identical economies with rigid wages and greedy governments. Each government wants to hold three-quarters of the global gold stock. If they pursue their targets independently, raising their interest rates competitively to attract capital inflows and gold, they will wind up with identical gold stocks but high unemployment rates. There are two ways to deal with this outcome. The two governments can agree to reduce their interest rates without even talking about their targets. That is the sort of 'policy barter' that many economists have in mind when they talk about policy-optimizing coordination. Alternatively, the governments can reveal and modify their targets. But what if they reveal them and then refuse to modify them? That is when conflicts or differences in targets obstruct coordination.

This case is too simple to be taken seriously – or is it? It does not differ from the case in which governments pursue incompatible current-account targets, and they seem to do that frequently. It does not differ from the case in which they attach different weights to various targets, including common or collective targets that they can pursue only at some sacrifice of national objectives. Problems can also arise when governments agree about the benefits of collective action but attach different weights to different domestic targets – when one government worries more about inflation than unemployment and the other takes the opposite view. They can be expected to disagree about the costs of acting jointly.

The fourth reason for the shortage of coordination applies to both varieties. Once again, however, it is more compelling when used to explain the scarcity of regime-preserving coordination. There are political and constitutional obstacles to every sort of international cooperation, but they are hardest to surmount when the costs are clear and the benefits less tangible. Each government will want to be a consumer of public goods without sharing the costs of producing them.

The political obstacles to policy coordination have been dramatized by the budgetary problems of the United States. How can the United States participate in international bargaining about fiscal policies when Congressional leaders can say that the President's budget is 'dead on arrival' at the top of Capitol Hill? There is an old story about the last days of World War I, when the German General Staff believed that the situation was serious but not hopeless and the Austrian General Staff thought that it was hopeless but not serious. The Viennese view may be more appropriate here. The budgetary deadlock of the mid-1980s does not signify permanent paralysis. Nor should we neglect the political problems faced by other major countries in making and adjusting fiscal policies:

> The political system in Japan has traditionally restrained the powers of the Prime Minister to a far greater degree than the US constitution limits the power of the American President. Always conscious of factional politics, the Prime Minister must answer to 'policy tribes,' which are groups of politicians committed to one-dimensional special interests. The Prime Minister must also placate vast armies of bureaucrats, not always from a position of strength. In Japan, it has often been said, politicians reign, but bureaucrats rule (Funabashi, 1988, p. 91).

The German situation is similar for different reasons:

Although the ruling coalition has no difficulty in obtaining sufficient parliamentary support for its taxing and spending priorities, in practice its control over fiscal policy is undermined by the following two factors. First, since the 1970s, . . . the SPD has received control of the Ministry of Finance, while the FDP has staffed the Ministry of Economics, an arrangement that has weakened the federal government's ability to undertake comprehensive or drastic measures. Second, the federal government controls less than 50 per cent of public investment, and only about 15 per cent of the nation's total public spending and investment, the remainder coming from the *Land* and local governments (ibid., p. 117).

There is, of course, a fundamental difference between these situations and the US situation. Once the German and Japanese governments have decided to make a policy change, they can commit themselves formally, and the US government cannot, because it cannot commit the Congress. Yet the record is not so very bad. President Carter was careful not to promise more than he could deliver – and he did deliver eventually. In another context, moreover, the White House obtained in advance a promise of rapid Congressional action on the trade-policy bargain produced by the Tokyo round of GATT negotiations – the 'fast track' that Congress would follow in agreeing to accept or reject those parts of the bargain requiring new legislation, and the new US administration should perhaps propose a similar stand-by arrangement as part of the fiscal-policy package it takes to Capitol Hill to break the budget deadlock.

The basic problems are political, not constitutional. No democratic government can make major policy changes without working hard to persuade the public that the new policies will be better than the old, if not indeed the best of all possible policies. When the time comes to coordinate policies, 'each national leader already has made a substantial investment in building a particular coalition at the domestic [game] board, and he or she will be loath to construct a different coalition simply to sustain an alternative policy mix that might be more acceptable internationally' (Putnam and Bayne, 1987, p. 11). In brief, fiscal policies are not very flexible in any democracy, regardless of its constitution.

Policy coordination is made more difficult by jurisdictional divisions within governments. The problem is most serious on the monetary side, especially in Germany and the United States, which have independent central banks. Here again, however, constitutional arrangements matter less than political realities, and independent central banks maintain their independence by being extremely astute politically. When they resist pressures from their governments, moreover, it is partly because they are more acutely aware of the way that interest-rate changes affect exchange rates. A unilateral change in German interest rates helped to precipitate the stock-market crash in October 1987, not because it was so significant by itself but because it provoked a strong reaction from Washington. On many more occasions, however, central banks have refused to adjust interest rates until they could be sure that foreign central banks were ready to move with them.[14]

Furthermore, monetary policies can be altered quickly and incrementally, without building a new political consensus. A change in monetary policy is usually the first indication of a change in official thinking about the economic outlook. Therefore, monetary policies can be coordinated more deftly than fiscal policies, despite jurisdictional difficulties in some countries.

The framework for policy coordination
Rigidities in the making of fiscal policies and differences of view about the ways in which they work are probably sufficient to account for the apparent shortage of policy-optimizing coordination – the governments' failure to exploit all of the potential gains. They may indeed account for a more important failure. Governments find it hard to optimize their policies, let alone engage in optimal coordination.

Quantitative studies of policy coordination need a benchmark – an operational representation of the non-cooperative equilibrium against which to measure the gains from coordination. They must therefore define fully optimal policies for each government acting unilaterally, and this is an instructive exercise. The welfare gains obtained by optimizing policies usually exceed the gains obtained thereafter by moving from non-cooperative to cooperative policies. Dealing with policy coordination between the United States and Europe, Hughes Hallett (1987) obtains these welfare measures:

Simulation	United States	Europe
Baseline	466.2	346.2
Non-cooperative	103.6	81.3
Cooperative	96.2	55.8

These are loss-function calculations, measuring the welfare costs of the governments' failure to reach their targets. Therefore, reductions are good things. But the biggest reductions occur on the way from the actual (baseline) situation to optimal non-cooperative policies, not from non-cooperative to cooperative (coordinated) policies. Political and institutional rigidities combine with the uncertainties of the real world to interfere with any sort of policy optimization.

The same rigidities and disagreements also help to account for the apparent shortage of regime-preserving coordination, and disagreements about targets are important too. They combine to produce disagreements about burden-sharing. Nevertheless, we can be moderately optimistic about the prospects for the particular sorts of coordination required to support exchange-rate management.

Recall the main points made in Chapter 3 about the policy instruments that should be used for exchange-rate management. Interest rates must be coordinated closely to influence capital flows and offset expectations of exchange-rate realignments. They cannot be assigned to that task exclusively, however, nor can fiscal policies be assigned exclusively to domestic objectives. On the one hand, fiscal policies affect current-account balances and, therefore, the task faced by monetary policies. On the other hand, fiscal policies cannot be adjusted frequently enough to stabilize aggregate demand, and some of that task passes to monetary policies.

Furthermore, exchange-rate management does not call for the rigid defence of pegged exchange rates within very narrow bands. The bands should be hard but wide, and central rates should be adjusted periodically to rectify disequilibria resulting from different inflation rates, real shocks, and imperfect policies. If fiscal policies cannot be adjusted often enough to avoid or correct external and internal imbalances, changes in exchange rates must take place more frequently.

It should be remembered, moreover, that international differences in fiscal policies do not necessarily destabilize exchange rates. They have not done so in the EMS, where they continue to be fairly large.[15] In fact, differences in fiscal policies can help to offset differences in savings rates that would otherwise produce current-account imbalances. The lesson to be learnt from the 1980s relates to the effects of large unilateral shifts in fiscal policies, which are bad news indeed.

The framework currently being developed for the multilateral surveillance of G-7 policies should be adapted to focus more sharply on fiscal policies. The process originated at the Versailles Summit of 1982, when the G-5 governments agreed to cooperate closely with the IMF in its own surveillance of exchange-rate policies. It was given more structure at the Tokyo Summit of 1986, when the task was reassigned from the G-5 to the G-7, and the governments agreed 'to review their individual economic objectives and forecasts collectively at least once a year ... with a particular view to examining their mutual compatibility' and to base that review on a list of quantitative indicators. It was refined again at the Venice Summit of 1987, when the list of indicators was pruned to six (growth rates of real GNP, inflation rates, budget balances, trade balances, interest rates, and exchange rates) and the aims of the exercise were stated more clearly. Attention was finally given to the need for governments to agree on policy objectives before they can appraise economic performance.[16]

Unfortunately, the G-7 governments are still far from any such agreement. They have been concentrating on a more technical problem – whether to rely on the governments' own numbers or those of the IMF. The issue is not trivial. Governments can be made to stand by their own numbers but are free to criticize or disavow all other numbers. Use of the Fund's numbers, however, would enhance its role in the actual analysis of policies – its ability to speak for the countries that consume the public goods produced by policy coordination. The interests of those countries must be represented forcefully as the G-7 governments gradually assume more responsibility for maintaining global economic stability, not merely for exchange-rate stability.

But other problems must be faced. The present list of indicators is less than satisfactory. It fails to distinguish clearly between targets and instruments, and the focus of the exercise is too narrow. It is concerned with the compatibility of national projections and policies rather than the quality of those policies.

Compatibility is vital for exchange-rate stability. If the fiscal policies of the G-7 governments look as though they will cause large current-account imbalances, monetary policies may be asked to produce large capital flows to cover the imbalances, and this may be impossible. The requisite flows may be too large for sustainability, and the requisite interest-rate differences may not be consistent with the maintenance of domestic economic stability in the individual G-7 countries. Fiscal policies have then to be adjusted by an *ad hoc* bargain or, more appropriately, by a standing commitment on the part of each government to integrate the results of multilateral surveillance into its own policy-making process at an early stage, before it has completed and announced its budget.

But compatibility is not enough. The G-7 governments must take responsibility for the most important public good, global economic stability, and the multilateral surveillance of their policies must emphasize quality, not merely compatibility. How will their policies affect the growth rate of global GNP? How will they affect commodity prices, interest rates, and other variables strategically important for all countries, but especially for the less-developed countries?

An omniscient policy-making body might look at the problem as a two-stage process:

The first stage should articulate and quantify composite policy objectives for the major industrial countries, relating to growth rates, inflation rates, and other variables. These should be framed as medium-term targets, but they should be updated and extended periodically. No attempt should be made to 'fine tune' the world, but the major industrial countries should not be allowed to pretend that they have no influence on – or responsibility for – the evolution of the world economy.

The second stage should translate the composite targets into operational commitments on the part of each participating government. Each country's obligations must be framed to take account of that country's special problems, but they should be consistent in two senses: (1) they should be adequate, taken together, to achieve the composite policy objectives; and (2) they should not involve larger changes in exchange rates than any other set of policy commitments capable of reaching the same objectives (Kenen, 1987b, p. 1453).

In this particular formulation, the exchange rate comes out at the end. In the rest of this paper, by contrast, exchange-rate stability was treated as the starting-point for policy coordination. But the two formulations are not very different in principle. Both emphasize the need to review exchange rates periodically to ask if realignments are needed. Furthermore, the current focus on exchange-rate stability must not divert the G-7 governments from concern with the global impact of their economic policies – the need to produce other public goods.

Policy coordination can never be perfected. If governments continue to pursue exchange-rate stability along lines recommended in this paper, central banks can be expected to coordinate interest-rate policies rather effectively, with some of the task being done tacitly as central banks pay more attention to exchange rates. But it is unrealistic to expect close or continuous coordination of fiscal policies. Budgetary politics and processes are too complicated. Nevertheless, an enduring commitment to exchange-rate stability should make governments more attentive to the external ramifications of their fiscal policies and help to defend the budgetary process from political and bureaucratic pressures. The prospects would improve, moreover, if multilateral surveillance focused clearly on the consequences of fiscal policies for the evolution of current-account balances and medium-term prospects for global economic growth. International consultations can have only marginal effects on national policies, but they may be more helpful than episodic bargaining about fiscal policies. Bargaining does not usually begin until large imbalances have built up and large changes in fiscal policies are needed to correct them.

Conclusion

Two questions remain: What would have happened in the early 1980s if there had been more intensive exchange-rate management? When should governments begin to move towards more durable exchange-rate arrangements?

Several economists have tried to show what various policy rules or guidelines might have done to improve economic performance in the 1980s.[17] They do not have much trouble, because their policy rules would have softened the sharp monetary contraction that occurred at the start of the decade and prevented the Reagan administration from running huge budget deficits.

It is harder to detect the influence of their exchange-rate rules, because those rules are not very strict and their influence is swamped by the improvements in monetary and fiscal policies. It would be particularly hard to simulate the influence of the exchange-rate regime proposed in this paper, which would have called for large amounts of intervention and would thus have had large effects on monetary conditions. At the start of this paper, moreover, I argued that exchange-rate regimes should be compared on the pessimistic supposition that all other policies will be imperfect. It would be wrong to compare the performance of floating exchange rates in the early 1980s under the influence of Reaganomics with the performance of managed exchange rates under more sensible fiscal policies.

The fiscal policies pursued by the United States would have caused serious trouble under any exchange-rate regime. But the symptoms would have been different under the arrangements proposed in this paper. The upward pressure on the dollar would have been limited by intervention, and if the intervention was not fully sterilized, it would have led to monetary contraction in Europe and Japan and monetary expansion in the United States.[18]

This point has been made by Frenkel (1987) and other economists critical of McKinnon's proposals for exchange-rate stabilization, and it is mentioned by Williamson and Miller (1987) as an objection to methods of exchange-rate management stricter than their own. But the resulting political pressures might have forced the US government to act earlier and more decisively on the budgetary front. At the same time, the monetary consequences of intervention would have given governments fair warning of the need to adjust exchange rates – to revalue the dollar but by less than it rose in the 1980s under the influence of market forces.

The new US administration will be urged to retreat from exchange-rate management and policy coordination. Writing shortly after the stock-market crash, Martin Feldstein put the case very bluntly:

Washington's explicit recognition of its responsibility for
America's economic future would ... reassure financial markets

that have become unnecessarily frightened by the prospect that international economic coordination will collapse.
Unfortunately, ever since the 1985 Plaza meeting, the administration and the governments of other industrial nations have emphatically asserted that international economic coordination is crucial to a healthy international economy in general and to continued US growth in particular. Since such assertions are not justified by the actual interdependence of the industrial economies, Americans have been inappropriately worried about whether coordination would continue.

Because foreign governments will inevitably pursue the policies that they believe are in their own best interests, it was inevitable that international coordination would eventually collapse ... But what contributed to the market decline was not the collapse of international macroeconomic coordination per se but the false impression created by governments that healthy expansion requires such coordination.

The US should now in a clear but friendly way end the international coordination of macroeconomic policy. We should continue to cooperate with other governments by exchanging information about current and future policy decisions, but we should recognize explicitly that Japan and Germany have the right to pursue the monetary and fiscal policies that they believe are in their own best interests.

It is frightening to the American public and upsetting to our financial markets to believe that the fate of our economy depends on the decisions made in Bonn and Tokyo. Portfolio investors, business managers and the public in general need to be reassured that we are not hostages to foreign economic policies, that the US is the master of its own economic destiny, and that our government can and will do what is needed to maintain healthy economic growth (Feldstein, 1987).

These views are held on both sides of the political divide, although they are rarely expressed so forcefully.[19] But they tend to reflect the economists' emphasis on policy-optimizing coordination and their corresponding neglect of the governments' concern with regime-preserving coordination. They also reflect the traditional US approach to the problem of symmetry – concern for the ability of the

United States to alter its exchange rate more freely than it could under the Bretton Woods System.

The United States has much to gain from exchange-rate management. The costs of large exchange-rate changes are very high. They may be even higher for the United States than for other countries, because nominal wages tend to be more rigid in the United States, giving the nominal exchange rate more influence over the real exchange rate.

But another, more immediate, consideration should influence the new US administration: the risk that the next exchange-rate cycle will begin as soon as the United States starts to deal with its budget deficit. That task must have the highest priority, for political as well as economic reasons, and international as well as domestic reasons. The new administration cannot hope to exercise leadership in international economic matters unless it moves promptly and decisively to cut the deficit. As soon as it does, however, the foreign-exchange market may start to change its mind about the dollar, and it may begin to appreciate.

The United States has another reason for investing political capital in the pursuit of exchange-rate stability. There has been a gradual decline in the relative importance of the dollar as an international currency, even as a reserve currency, and this trend is likely to continue. Yet foreign holdings of dollar assets are larger than ever. Some of those holdings are firmly lodged, but massive amounts could be dislodged by exchange-rate movements and the resulting capital flows would amplify those movements.

The other G-7 countries have equally strong interests in exchange-rate stability. Japan has begun to adjust comprehensively to the prospect of a strong yen over the long term. The economic and political costs of reversing that adjustment would be very high. In Europe, monetary integration will reduce but not eliminate the internal tensions resulting from large changes in the value of the dollar. Finally, Japan and Europe have reason to fear a recrudescence of protectionist pressures in the United States, the most predictable consequence of another large exchange-rate swing.

The costs of exchange-rate management are not negligible, but the largest costs are the costs of failure, which would assuredly result in a reversion to insular attitudes and policies. The benefits of successful management make that cost worth risking. Successful management over the long term, however, calls for the consolidation and further articulation of present informal arrangements. There is no need for a new Bretton Woods, but there is the need to reaffirm clearly and promptly the commitment to monetary cooperation embodied in the Louvre agreement.

APPENDIX

This appendix provides empirical support for two statements in the text. The first concerns the state of expectations in the foreign-exchange market at the start of 1988, when central-bank intervention proved to be unusually effective. The second concerns the record of the EMS in realigning exchange rates without giving the market a one-way speculative option.*

The state of expectations

In its monthly *Forex Survey*, Smith New Court Far East provides a compilation of exchange-rate forecasts made by individual foreign-exchange traders. In Table A.1, I show the standard deviations of those forecasts expressed as percentages of the average forecasts. My method is easily illustrated by looking at the forecasts of the DM/$ rate for the end of December 1987 made at the end of November 1987. This was the array of forecasts in DM per dollar:

Exchange rate	Number of forecasts
1.58	3
1.60	3
1.61	1
1.62	4
1.64	2
1.65	2

*I thank Enzio von Pfeil for supplying the data used in the first part of this appendix and answering my questions about them. I am grateful to Judith Kleinman for help with the computations reported in the second part.

Table A.1 An analysis of foreign-exchange forecasts

Standard deviations of forecasts as percentages of average forecasts	DM/$	¥/$
Forecasts for end December 1988:		
At end September 1987	10.48	12.53
At end October 1987	9.99	13.04
At end November 1987	9.22	8.22
At end December 1987	8.80	11.12
At end January 1988	5.50	6.87
At end February 1988	5.48	6.61
At end March 1988	5.25	6.83
Short-term forecasts:		
End September 1987 for end December 1987	3.59	4.26
End October 1987 for end December 1987	3.67	5.03
End November 1987 for end December 1987	1.52	2.00
End December 1987 for end March 1988	4.53	6.77
End January 1988 for end March 1988	2.93	3.69
End February 1988 for end March 1988	1.83	2.09
End March 1988 for end June 1988	2.47	2.90

Source: Calculated from monthly compilations of individual forecasts distributed by Smith New Court Far East. Compilations of forecasts made in September and October 1987 cover 11 individual forecasts; those made thereafter cover between 13 and 16 forecasts.

The average forecast was 1.61 DM per dollar, and the standard deviation was 2.45 pfennigs per dollar, or 1.52 per cent of the average forecast. The figures in Table A.1 have four interesting features:

(1) The standard deviations for the DM/$ forecasts are uniformly smaller than those for the ¥/$ forecasts.

(2) The standard deviations of the DM/$ forecasts for the fixed date December 1988 decline monotonically as the forecast interval shortens; those of the ¥/$ do so less regularly, and there is a big jump at the end of 1987.

(3) A similar tendency is visible within each group of short-term forecasts, but the two-month forecasts made at the end of October 1987, just after the stock-market crash, have higher standard deviations than the three-month forecasts made at the end of September 1987.

Appendix

(4) The standard deviations for the forecasts made at the end of December 1987 are larger than those for the two other pairs of three-month forecasts (those made at the end of September 1987 and at the end of March 1988).

The points made at (2) and (4) about the forecasts made in December 1987 support the assertion in Chapter 3 that there was much uncertainty about exchange-rate trends even though the market was predicting a further fall in the dollar. (The average forecast for the DM/$ rate predicted a 4 per cent depreciation in the first quarter of 1988, and the average forecast for the ¥/$ rate predicted a 5 per cent depreciation.)

Realignments in the EMS

When a pegged exchange rate is revalued or devalued by an amount larger than the width of the band surrounding it, the new and old bands cannot overlap, and the market exchange rate has to change. Market participants are given a one-way speculative option. Table A.2 reviews the record of the EMS, asking how well it has done in realigning exchange rates without offering that option. The first column reports results for all 7 currencies participating in the EMS exchange-rate mechanism. The second column omits changes in the bands for bilateral exchange rates involving the Italian lira, which are wider than the others.

Table A.2 An analysis of EMS realignments

Category	All currencies	Excluding Italian lira
(1) Number of realignments	11	11
(2) Possible changes in bilateral central rates[a]	231	165
(3) Actual changes in bilateral central rates[b]	137	94
(4) Changes smaller than width of band[c]	99	56
(5) Changes larger than width of band	38	38
(6) Small changes as percentage of possible	43	34
(7) Small changes as percentage of actual	72	60

Source: Original computations based on changes in ECU central rates given in Ungerer et al. (1987), Table 8 (which are more precise than the figures shown in Table 2.2).

a. With 7 currencies in the exchange-rate mechanism, there are 21 bilateral central rates, and these were realigned 11 times.

b. Excludes those instances in which the bilateral rate did not change because neither of the ECU central rates was changed.

c. Includes instances in which the change equalled the width of the band.

Line (1) shows the number of exchange-rate realignments. Line (2) shows the number of changes in bilateral central rates and bands that would have taken place if each realignment had changed at least 6 of the ECU central rates and thus changed every bilateral band. (Since there are 7 currencies in the exchange-rate mechanism, there are 21 bilateral central rates and bands, and there were 11 realignments, giving 231 as the largest possible number of changes in the bilateral rates and bands.) Line (3) shows the actual number of changes in bilateral central rates and bands, and the next two lines classify those changes. Thus, 99 of the 137 changes in bilateral central rates were smaller than the width of the corresponding band and thus small enough to deprive the market of a one-way speculative option. The last two lines of the table summarize the outcomes. Line (6) shows the number of small changes as a percentage of possible changes (e.g., 99 : 231 = 0.43). Line (7) shows the number of small changes as a percentage of actual changes (e.g., 99 : 137 = 0.72). These are the 'successes' reported in Chapter 3. It should be noted that all of the changes would have been 'small' if all of the bands had been as wide as those for the Italian lira.

NOTES

Chapter 2

1 I borrow from Keynes (1936, p. 156), who compared professional investment with competitions that are won by guessing which of a hundred faces will be chosen as prettiest by the largest number of competitors 'so that each competitor has to pick, not those faces which he himself finds prettiest, but those which he thinks likeliest to catch the fancy of the other competitors, all of whom are looking at the problem from the same point of view. It is not a case of choosing those which . . . are really the prettiest, nor even those which average opinion genuinely thinks the prettiest. We have reached the third degree where we devote our intelligences to anticipating what average opinion expects the average opinion to be.'

2 Dornbusch and Frankel (1987) point out that these models did not represent state-of-the art analysis twenty years ago; economists were well aware of their flaws. But the models that inform – or misinform – discussions about policy, even by professional economists, are not the models used in current teaching and research; they are simplified versions of older models, which are widely understood and thus facilitate communication.

3 See, e.g., de Vries (1987), who argues that it was not difficult to rectify imbalances between aggregate demand (absorption) and aggregate supply (income), which is the essence of current-account adjustment. Aggregate supply was growing rapidly and it was thus sufficient to reduce the growth rate of aggregate demand until supply caught up; it was not necessary to cut the level of demand. There is some truth to this view, and it sharpens the contrast between adjustment in the

1950s and 1960s on the one hand and in the 1970s and 1980s on the other. But those who had to manage aggregate demand in that 'golden era' would be quick to caution that it was not easy.

4 This was the dilemma posed by Triffin (1960); it was the underlying rationale for the First Amendment to the Articles of Agreement of the IMF, on the creation and use of Special Drawing Rights (SDRs).

5 We owe this formulation to Mundell (1969), although the problem was understood earlier, as indicated in the text below.

6 Its concurrence was not required if the change, together with all previous changes, would alter the member's par value by no more than 10 per cent of its initial value, and it had to concur in any other change proposed by a member if the change was needed to correct a fundamental disequilibrium. (That term, however, was not defined in the Articles of Agreement.) A member that changed its par value despite the Fund's objections was barred automatically from drawing on the Fund, unless granted an exception.

7 When working through this political arithmetic, remember that all three exchange rates were pegged, so that a revaluation of the mark would necessarily raise its value in terms of the dollar, not merely in terms of the franc. That is not true now; a revaluation of the mark within the EMS does not necessarily raise its value in terms of the dollar. The three episodes cited in this paragraph are described at length in Solomon (1982), chs. 3, 5, and 9.

8 See Solomon (1982), chs. 10–13, for an account of these developments, including the debates within the US government that led it to adopt a confrontational approach.

9 The Committee was established in keeping with the Smithsonian Agreement, which said that 'discussions should be promptly undertaken, particularly in the framework of the IMF, to consider reform of the international monetary system' and that 'attention should be directed to the appropriate monetary means and division of responsibilities for defending stable exchange rates and for insuring a proper degree of convertibility'. The first comprehensive proposal for reform was made by Secretary Shultz in September 1972; it assumed that most countries would want to peg their exchange rates but included floating as an option. A communiqué issued by the Committee days after the float began said that 'the exchange rate regime should remain based on stable but adjustable par values' but that 'floating rates could provide a useful technique in particular situations'. Similar language appeared in the *Outline of Reform* published some months later. On the work of the Committee, see Solomon (1982), ch. 14, and Williamson (1977, 1982).

10 This interpretation draws on Kenen (1973).

11 For a detailed account of the issues and motives that led to the Plaza and Louvre agreements, see Funabashi (1988).

12 See, e.g., Balladur (1988), although his proposals are more imaginative than those which used to come from Paris.

13 See, e.g., Giavazzi and Pagano (1986), Melitz (1987), and Tsoukalis (1987). Tsoukalis rightly notes that the actual gains from EMS membership, viewed from this standpoint, have been less impressive than was the force of the argument on the incentive to join; see also Collins (1988) and Artis and Taylor (1988).

14 The interest in a European central bank also reflects another worrisome concern, that the abolition of capital controls required to complete the common market by 1992 will undermine the stability of the EMS unless it is transformed into a system of permanently fixed exchange rates. Capital controls are discussed in Chapter 4.

15 See, e.g., Dominguez (1986a), Frankel and Froot (1986, 1987), and Krugman (1988a); recent research on this issue is surveyed by Dornbusch and Frankel (1987).

16 The combination of flexible asset prices with sticky goods prices can also cause the nominal exchange rate to overshoot its long-run equilibrium in response to a disturbance or policy change; see Dornbusch (1976). But the exchange-rate swing of the 1980s, discussed below, cannot be explained that way. It was too large and long.

17 This theme is developed more fully by Krugman (1988a), drawing partly on work by Dixit (1987) concerning the effects of uncertainty about the future exchange rate. A firm that has made the investment required to enter a market may stay in that market when the exchange rate turns against it, even though it cannot cover its variable costs, if it is uncertain about the permanence of the new exchange rate. Conversely, a firm that has left the market may not make the investment required to re-enter it when the exchange rate moves in its favour. Costs of entry and re-entry combine with exchange-rate variability to reduce the firms' responsiveness to the current exchange rate. For more on the allocational effects of the exchange-rate swing, see Marris (1987), pp. 54–60.

Chapter 3

1 Frenkel and Goldstein (1986) use similar questions to organize their analysis of target zones, and I have borrowed some of their answers as well.

2 A systematic treatment of the possibilities would also look at currency unification. It is being discussed actively in Europe (see, e.g., Gros and Thygesen, 1988) and has been proposed in one form or another for the whole group of industrial countries. A gold standard or McKinnon's gold standard without gold would go far in that

direction, and Cooper (1984) goes even further, calling for central-bank unification. I do not examine those proposals here, however, because they are not realistic options for the next decade, except in Europe, and I have discussed the issues elsewhere; see Kenen (1969, 1976) and Allen and Kenen (1980).

3 The effectiveness of the Plaza Communiqué has been challenged by Feldstein (1986) and others, because the dollar had started to depreciate earlier, and its path did not change sharply after the Communiqué. But the dollar looked to be levelling out in the weeks before the Communiqué and dropped abruptly after it; see Funabashi (1988), pp. 22–4 and 217–19. (Taken in isolation, the Plaza and Louvre agreements can be viewed as instances of episodic management. Taken jointly and in conjunction with subsequent events, they represent a rather systematic approach.)

4 The December statement was much like its predecessor. It drew attention to policies already adopted rather than announcing new ones, and the operative statement about exchange rates was similar to the passage quoted in Chapter 2, although more guarded. (It said that the governments would 'cooperate closely on exchange markets', but did not promise 'to foster stability of exchange rates around current levels'.)

5 The Canadian authorities have followed this strategy frequently, but the strongly regressive character of expectations about the Canadian dollar has probably protected them from perverse expectational effects.

6 The weights used to calculate effective rates derive from the other countries' shares in the merchandise trade of the country concerned or from their shares in world trade. The IMF uses a more sophisticated weighting scheme, which allows explicitly for the sensitivity of a country's current account to each exchange rate included in its effective rate.

7 If Williamson's aim was to stabilize *all* exchange rates, parallel movements of US, German, and Japanese policies would be appropriate; they would help to stabilize the dollar, mark, and yen against the peso. Since he is concerned instead to stabilize the *key* rates, parallel movements are less appropriate. (An appreciation of the peso could, of course, be offset by reducing the effective central rate for the dollar, which would obviate the need for any change in US policies. But that starts to take us out of Williamson's framework, based on effective rates, back towards a more conventional framework, based on bilateral rates.)

8 See Krugman and Baldwin (1987) and Krugman (1988a). The problem of lags, much discussed in the exchange-rate literature, is less important here, because the relevant notion of equilibrium pertains to the medium or long run, when lags have worked themselves out.

9 See Williamson (1985), Frenkel and Goldstein (1986), Williamson and Miller (1987), and Kenen (1988).

10 See Gros and Thygesen (1988) for more description and discussion. Governments proposing realignments have usually offered or been obliged to make changes in domestic policies; see Ungerer, et al. (1986), Table 10.

11 See Crockett and Goldstein (1987) for a broader and less negative view of these and other indicators. The use of indicators for policy surveillance is discussed in Chapter 6, below.

12 Gros and Thygesen (1988) take a different view regarding real exchange rates within the EMS, believing that the requisite adjustments can be made by changing domestic prices and wages rather than nominal exchange rates.

13 The 'divergence indicator' adopted initially by the EMS was a rate-based indicator, but it has not worked well; see Ungerer, et al. (1986). Use of a reserve-based indicator was discussed extensively by the Committee of Twenty; see IMF (1974). For a comparison between reserve-based and rate-based indicators, see Kenen (1975), where I showed that an indicator based on the level of reserves is far inferior to one based on the change in reserves, while indicators based on changes in reserves and on moving averages of actual exchange rates have rather similar properties.

14 This formulation seems 'harder' than those in earlier versions (e.g., Williamson, 1985), which surrounded the bands by 'soft buffers' and put less stress on intervention. But intervention and interest-rate policy switch places midway through the present version, where main reliance is placed on interest-rate policy, 'which should be supplemented, or at times might even be replaced, by the use of intervention in the foreign exchange markets' (Williamson and Miller, 1987, p. 15).

15 This is an important corollary to the point made by Dixit (1987) and developed by Krugman (1988a) that highly variable exchange rates tend to lose their influence on decisions about market entry and exit.

16 The same point is made by Williamson and Miller (1987), p. 61. In fact, most of the reasons given here for favouring wide bands appear in their list too.

17 A wide band has another helpful consequence. If the lira is *not* devalued, those who sold it can take losses, and their size will increase with the width of the band. In the example given above, they can take a 12 per cent loss if the lira rises to the top of its band, but this loss would be cut in half it the band were cut in half. The wider the band, moreover, the easier it is to realign exchange rates *before* they reach their limits. If the lira had started at the centre of its band, it could

have been devalued by as much as 6 per cent without forcing the market rate to move with the central rate.

18 This statement covers eight of the G-10 countries plus Switzerland. (Canada is omitted because it had a floating rate for part of the period, and the United States is omitted because its currency was the numeraire.) There were only 7 changes in that 20-year period, and the smallest were the 5 per cent revaluations of the German mark and Dutch guilder in 1961. Those larger than 12 per cent were the devaluations of the French franc in 1958 and 1969 and the devaluation of the pound in 1967.

19 The first point is developed in Kenen (1986), where I argued that countries cannot always make the best use of IMF resources because most drawings on the Fund must be repaid rather rapidly. The second point is developed in Kenen (1987a) in conjunction with the theory of policy coordination.

20 See Dornbusch (1988) and Krugman (1988a). Simulations by Currie and Wren-Lewis (1988) support their view; feedback rules based on the Williamson-Miller framework do better than rules that use fiscal policies to regulate current-account balances and monetary policies to regulate aggregate demand.

21 See Kenen (1987a).

22 See Hodrick and Srivastava (1984), Hsieh (1984), and the survey by Levich (1985).

23 These possibilities are raised in recent work by Dominguez (1986a) and Collins (1987). Frankel and Froot (1987) have used survey data instead but have not been much more successful in isolating the risk premium one would expect to find if foreign and domestic assets were imperfect substitutes.

24 See Obstfeld (1983) and Blundell-Wignall and Masson (1985).

25 See Loopesko (1983), Lewis (1986), and Dominguez (1986b), whose work suggests that sterilized intervention is effective when the central bank's monetary policy lends credibility to its exchange-rate policy. Central banks appear to have offset changes in their holdings of reserves by changing their holdings of domestic assets; see, e.g., Mastropasqua, et al. (1988), who find that the German authorities have typically offset more than 60 per cent of changes in reserves, while the French and Italians have offset between 25 and 40 per cent. But these are not conclusive findings, nor do they bear directly on the effectiveness of sterilized intervention. If foreign and domestic assets were perfect substitutes, a change in domestic assets would automatically induce an equal but opposite change in foreign assets, and this would look like sterilization. We must be able to distinguish cause from effect before we can draw strong conclusions from these findings.

Chapter 4

1 Persson (1987) provides an introduction and critique.

2 Taken to its logical conclusion, the Barro-Gordon model restates the fundamental proposition of the 'new' macroeconomics – that monetary policy cannot affect the real economy – but casts it as a long-run tendency. If a government protects its reputation by keeping its promises, it can never alter output or employment. If it risks its reputation by breaking its promises, it will gradually lose its ability to surprise the private sector. Rogoff (1985) uses the same framework to show why international policy coordination can be counterproductive, but his results have been challenged by Currie, et al. (1987) and by Carraro and Giavazzi (1988).

3 In technical terms, the government must constrain itself to choose among the subset of future policies that are completely 'time consistent', meaning that policies promised today must be no less attractive tomorrow, when the time comes to implement them. The government must not make promises that affect the behaviour of the private sector in ways that may tempt the government to break its promises.

4 This term is used by Putnam and Bayne (1987), who criticize economists for worrying too much about cheating and for treating it as one of the main obstacles to international cooperation. If there is too little cooperation, they say, it is because governments want to keep their promises and worry about their ability to do so, not because they fear that their partners will cheat.

5 Bryant (1987) has applied this argument to the problems of time consistency and reneging. He points out that all policy announcements are contingent on forecasts about the state of the world, explicitly or implicitly, which makes it impossible for anyone to know whether a government is reneging on previous promises or adapting to new circumstances. See also Kenen (1987a).

6 See, e.g., Gros and Thygesen (1988). It should be noted, moreover, that there were no more realignments in 1987 despite the financial turbulence that developed later in the year.

7 Writing in *The Observer* on 4 October 1987, William Keegan reported that 'these ranges are believed to be Yen 139 to Yen 153 to the dollar (central rate Yen 146) and DM1.75 to DM1.90 to the dollar (central rate DM1.825).' Williamson and Miller (1987, p. 67) warned that the bands were too narrow and that the central rates were probably inappropriate, but they were optimistic about the viability of the Louvre Accord. 'The soft buffers of the Louvre reference ranges, the apparent pro tem. quality of the agreed targets, and the failure to publish the ranges, will all make it relatively easy to beat a graceful retreat when the time comes.'

8 The governments themselves had detailed discussions about the rates and bands, but they did not always agree about the implications. They did apparently agree that the bands were to be soft. See Funabashi (1988), ch. 8, especially pp. 183–7.

9 See, e.g., Krugman (1988b) and Feldstein (1987).

10 Funabashi (1988), pp. 188–9.

11 Krugman is alert to these dangers; see Krugman (1987), where he describes the extended time in which the rate stays in its band as a 'target zone honeymoon'.

12 At times, governments have been the victims of their own credibility. In the early 1960s, the US authorities intervened on the forward foreign-exchange market to influence the profitability of capital movements. But they could not drive the forward rates beyond the spot-rate bands, because those bands were hard and were not expected to shift.

13 See Krugman (1979).

14 See, e.g., Obstfeld (1984), Flood and Garber (1984), and Grilli (1986). For applications to the EMS, see Driffill (1988) and Obstfeld (1988). The point stressed in the text below, that the market can generate a self-fulfilling crisis without any help from the government, is made in Obstfeld (1986).

15 See Masera (1987) and Mastropasqua, et al. (1988).

16 On the effectiveness of these controls, see Giavazzi and Giovannini (1987), Artis and Taylor (1988), and Mastropasqua, et al. (1988). These studies compare the behaviour of onshore and offshore interest rates for assets denominated in a common currency. In the absence of capital controls, interest rates should be the same on comparable assets, but they have differed systematically in the French and Italian cases while becoming more alike in the UK and Japanese cases, where capital controls have been eliminated.

17 The rapid reversal of capital flows has been reflected clearly in movements of reserves; see Melitz and Michel (1988).

18 For details, see Micossi (1985) and Masera (1987).

19 From March 1979 through June 1987, gross intervention at the margins amounted to $58.3 billion, and total intervention in EMS currencies amounted to $219.4 billion. Drawings on the very short-term financing facility (VSTF) amounted to $42.2 billion. Therefore, they financed 72 per cent of intervention at the margins but only 19 per cent of total intervention in EMS currencies (Mastropasqua, et al., 1988, Table 3).

Chapter 5

1 Strictly speaking, governments do not borrow from the IMF; they use their own national currencies to purchase foreign currencies. But they

must pay service charges and repurchase their own currencies, so drawings are very similar to borrowings.

2 This classification has been used before; see the references in Kenen (1983a). I draw on that paper heavily here.

3 There are two exceptions to this generalization. The use of the yen in invoicing Japanese exports has been rather small, although it is growing rapidly, and the US dollar is more important than the Canadian dollar in invoicing third countries' exports to Canada. In the case of exports to the United States, moreover, the dollar is used more often than the exporting country's currency. In Kenen (1983a), I estimated the percentages of other countries' exports that appear to be invoiced in dollars:

	Importer	
Exporter	*United States*	*Other countries*
Belgium	57	10
France	45	8
Germany	34	3
Italy	46	27
Japan	89	75
Netherlands	68	11
United Kingdom	52	12

These figures refer to 1979–80, and it would be hard to update them. But the use of the dollar to invoice Japanese exports has presumably fallen because the yen is used more heavily.

4 International Monetary Fund, *International Financial Statistics*, March 1987.

5 Bank for International Settlements, *Annual Report*, 1987, cited hereafter as BIS (1987).

6 See Group of Thirty (1982), which collates answers to a questionnaire distributed to central banks and concludes that the dollar is the 'only intervention currency for all practical purposes' (p. 4).

7 Mastropasqua, et al. (1988), Table 3; intramarginal intervention in EMS currencies includes $9 billion of intervention in ECU.

8 Figures for 1986 from BIS (1987) include banks in all major centres; figures for earlier years from Kenen (1983a) include only European banks. The numbers themselves are defined rather arbitrarily. Since they cover the banks' foreign-currency claims, not their total claims, dollar claims of US banks are excluded but DM claims are included, while dollar claims of German banks are included and DM claims are excluded. The numbers cannot be used to put the whole picture together. Furthermore, the figures are affected by exchange-rate

changes, and the recent decline in the share of the dollar is due partly to the depreciation of the dollar. But that is not the whole story; the share of the dollar was higher in 1981 than in 1986, although dollar exchange rates were similar in those two years.

9 Figures for 1984–6 from BIS (1987) over all international issues; earlier figures from Kenen (1983a) cover only Eurobond issues.

10 See Krugman (1980) and Chrystal (1987).

11 They were less tightly constrained under the Bretton Woods System, when they were free in principle to cash in their dollars for gold. But they were not free to do so in practice. Each one was large enough to fear that its actions would trigger similar actions by others and force the United States to abandon the fixed price for gold.

12 Germany takes a similar stance within the EMS. The rules of the EMS are designed to make it more symmetrical than the Bretton Woods System. Germany must intervene when the mark reaches the limit of its band vis-à-vis some other EMS currency. But it usually leaves intramarginal intervention to its partners. See Mastropasqua, et al. (1988), Table 4.

13 Data on reserves and intervention from International Monetary Fund, *International Financial Statistics* (various issues), and Board of Governors of the Federal Reserve System, *Federal Reserve Bulletin*, April 1988. Like many other numbers in this chapter, however, these are affected by exchange-rate changes. Thus, the increase in German and Japanese reserves overstates their intervention, because the depreciation of the dollar raised the dollar value of their non-dollar reserves. US data on the dollar holdings of all foreign governments show that they rose by a total of $81 billion in 1986 and 1987, which was not much more than the increase in German and Japanese reserves and thus fails to account for the known increase in other countries' dollar holdings. (The US numbers understate the increase in total dollar holdings by omitting dollars held in the Eurocurrency market. Nevertheless, there would appear to be a large gap somewhere in the data.)

14 The Treasury holds its foreign-currency reserves in its Exchange Stabilization Fund (ESF). When the ESF sells marks for dollars, it uses the dollars to buy US government securities, which does not reduce the total stock of debt but reduces the stock held by the public.

15 The foreign assets of the Bundesbank rose by DM30.9 billion in 1987, and the supply of central-bank money rose by DM16.8 billion or 9.2 per cent, twice the annual average for the five previous years (International Monetary Fund, *International Financial Statistics*, various issues).

16 These arrangements were not put in place to finance US intervention; there was little of that in the 1960s. They were used to shift exchange-rate risks temporarily. The United States drew foreign currencies to

buy back dollars from foreign central banks. But other governments used the swap arrangements to acquire dollars when they were needed for intervention. See Solomon (1982), chs. 3, 5, and 6.

17 See Kenen (1983b) for proposals to make the SDR a more useful reserve asset by promoting its use in private markets, and Kenen (1986) for proposals to make the IMF more flexible and influential. The more modest proposals made later in the text are not inconsistent with these long-run objectives.

18 Under Art. V.2(b) of the Articles of Agreement, the IMF may perform financial services for its members that do not involve its own accounts. The creation of a substitution account would not require an amendment.

19 Under the 1987 Basle-Nyborg agreement, there is a 'presumption' favouring their use to finance intramarginal intervention, but only in limited amounts and on stricter conditions regarding repayment; see Masera (1987).

20 This particular argument is weak, however, because interest rates tend to reflect the market's exchange-rate expectations; when the market expects the dollar to depreciate, interest rates on foreign-currency debt will be lower than interest rates on dollar debt, and foreign-currency borrowing can reduce the cost of servicing the debt even if the dollar does depreciate.

21 Purchases by Americans might be minimized if foreign-currency bonds were issued only in very large denominations. American financial institutions large enough to buy them might not be particularly interested, having already learned to deal in foreign-currency instruments. But some large institutions might still be interested, because they could trade US Treasury issues conveniently and use them to satisfy legal and conventional restrictions that cannot be met by holding foreign-currency instruments issued by foreign entities.

22 These negotiations are described in Solomon (1982), ch. 15; the mechanics of the proposal itself are analysed in Kenen (1981), which also traces its antecedents. The arrangements for issuing the SDR claims are similar in principle to those for issuing ECU in the EMS, and the broader proposal made later in the text resembles them even more closely, because it would substitute an SDR claim for both gold and dollars. The arrangements for issuing ECU are described in Micossi (1985).

23 The larger figure reflects the fact that the dollar itself makes up about 40 per cent of the SDR. The other constituent currencies are the mark, pound, yen, and French franc.

24 Recall the figures quoted earlier. The United States had about $35 billion of currency reserves and liquid claims on the IMF *plus* $27 billion in credit lines under the swap agreements with the G-7 countries, Switzerland, and the BIS, *plus* $5 billion of readily usable

drawing rights under its IMF quota. If the swap lines were doubled to $54 billion, and 90 million ounces of gold were exchanged for SDR claims worth about $28 billion, the total would rise to $122 billion.

Chapter 6

1 Similar definitions are used by Bryant (1980, p. 465), Artis and Ostry (1986, p. 75), and Frankel (1987b). The varieties of cooperation are discussed in Kenen (1987a), on which I draw frequently in this chapter. Other authors are less emphatic about instruments in their definitions of coordination. Without those commitments, however, the concept becomes too elastic. At the start of the 1980s, governments agreed firmly to combat inflation but did not agree on the instruments that they should use to do so. Chapter 2 described the outcome – huge movements in real exchange rates and current-account balances. No one would want to identify that outcome with policy coordination.

2 See, e.g., Putnam and Bayne (1987), ch. 4.

3 I have drawn this distinction elsewhere (Kenen, 1987a, 1987b, 1988), using different rubrics to describe the two approaches. It should not be confused with the distinction drawn later between the consistency and quality of policies, both of which pertain to the public-goods approach.

4 Following Hamada (1974, 1976), the Nash and Pareto equilibria are usually depicted with the aid of reaction curves; see, e.g., Cooper (1985), Eichengreen (1985), and Artis and Ostry (1986). Reaction curves appear to say that governments respond directly to changes in other governments' policies. If that were the case, however, the Nash equilibrium would tend to break down; each government would soon notice that other governments do not stand pat when it alters its own policies. Therefore, reaction curves should be deemed to say that governments respond to the *effects* of their partners' policies. They can then be expected to react repeatedly without drawing any inference about policy interdependence. For surveys of research reflecting the policy-optimizing approach, see Cooper (1985), Kenen (1987a), and Fischer (1988); for a more thorough review of recent theoretical developments, see Oudiz and Sachs (1985).

5 See, e.g., Buiter and Eaton (1985) and Eichengreen (1985).

6 Cooper (1985) and Kindleberger (1986) are prominent among the economists; for the views of political scientists and policy-makers, see Putnam and Bayne (1987), ch. 1, and the sources cited there.

7 Strictly speaking, it becomes an intermediate objective, adopted to defend each national economy and the international economic system against the effects of exchange-rate instability.

8 See, e.g., Canzoneri and Gray (1985) and McKibbin and Sachs (1986). This view resembles the political argument for exchange-rate pegging

set out in Chapter 2 and is open to the same objection; governments will not subscribe to rules that constrain their behaviour unless they want to tie their own hands – and will not want to do that permanently. There is a different welfare-maximizing case for exchange-rate pegging when foreign and domestic assets are imperfect substitutes. If exchange rates are pegged, each government, acting unilaterally, can respond in a fully optimal way to various disturbances; if exchange rates float, it cannot do so. Exchange-rate changes interfere with the pursuit of price stability. Like most theoretical conclusions, however, this one depends on a number of restrictive assumptions; see Kenen (1987a).

9 This list draws on Frankel (1987b).

10 Quoted in Putnam and Henning (1986), p. 100.

11 Some of these disagreements, however, may mask disagreements about objectives. It may be more convenient for governments to say 'That won't work' than to say 'We don't like that'. If the disagreements are about objectives, however, they are more serious obstacles to regime-preserving coordination that to policy-optimizing coordination. We shall soon see that differences in national objectives can actually enhance the potential gains from policy-optimizing coordination.

12 Three are ruled out because Europe would be worse off on the US view of the world, eight are ruled out because the United States would be worse off on the European view, and the other nine are ruled out because both parties would be worse off on the other's view.

13 These numbers are not strictly comparable with the 40 per cent failure rate reported by Frankel and Rockett, which covered all ten models. The corresponding rate for the six models used by Holtham and Hughes Hallett was about 38 per cent.

14 See Funabashi (1988), chs. 2 and 7. But his assessment of monetary cooperation (pp. 209–10) is more critical than mine. He interprets the central bankers' silence at certain G-5 meetings as reflecting a reluctance to coordinate monetary policies. It should perhaps be seen as reflecting their reluctance to endorse the rather vague commitments made by finance ministers – commitments that the central banks would have to implement eventually, risking their own credibility.

15 See Gros and Thygesen (1988), p. 7.

16 The origins and evolution of this framework are described by Putnam and Bayne (1987), ch. 9, and Funabashi (1988), ch. 6.

17 See, e.g., Williamson and Miller (1987) and Currie and Wren-Lewis (1988).

18 Monetary expansion would have taken place in the United States even without any major change in institutional arrangements. If foreign central banks had conducted most of the intervention, they would have run down their dollar reserves and sold US government

securities. If the US Treasury had conducted some of the intervention, the ESF would have sold US government securities to finance its purchases of foreign currencies. US interest rates would have risen in both cases, forcing the Federal Reserve to make open-market purchases and thus raise the growth rate of the money supply. (If the Federal Reserve had conducted some of the intervention, the US money supply would have risen automatically.)

19 See Dornbusch (1988), and Krugman (1988b), and Fischer (1988, p. 36), who says that 'there would be little need for coordination if each country were taking good care of its domestic policies'.

REFERENCES

Allen, P.R., and P.B. Kenen (1980). *Asset Markets, Exchange Rates, and Economic Integration*, Cambridge, Cambridge University Press.

Artis, M.J., and S. Ostry (1986). *International Economic Policy Coordination*, Chatham House Papers, London, Royal Institute of International Affairs.

Artis, M.J., and M.P. Taylor (1988). 'Exchange Rates and the EMS: Assessing the Track Record,' in F. Giavazzi, S. Micossi, and M. Miller, eds., *The European Monetary System*, Cambridge, Cambridge University Press.

Balladur, E. (1988). 'Rebuilding an International Monetary System,' *The Wall Street Journal*, 23 February.

Barro, R.J., and D. Gordon (1983). 'Rules, Discretion, and Reputation in a Model of Monetary Policy,' *Journal of Monetary Economics*, 12, July.

Blundell-Wignall, A., and P.R. Masson (1985). 'Exchange Rate Dynamics and Intervention Rules,' *IMF Staff Papers*, 32, March.

Bryant, R.C. (1980). *Money and Monetary Policy in Interdependent Nations*, Washington, The Brookings Institution.

—— (1987). 'Intergovernment Coordination of Economic Policies,' in P.B. Kenen, ed., *International Monetary Cooperation: Essays in Honor of Henry C. Wallich*, Essays in International Finance 169, Princeton, International Finance Section, Princeton University.

Buiter, W.H., and J. Eaton (1985). 'Policy Decentralization and Exchange Rate Management in Interdependent Economies,' in J.S. Bhandari, ed., *Exchange Rate Management under Uncertainty*, Cambridge, MIT Press.

Canzoneri, M.B., and J.A. Gray (1985). 'Monetary Policy Games and the Consequences of Noncooperative Behavior,' *International Economic Review*, 26, October.

Carraro, C., and F. Giavazzi (1988). 'Can International Policy Coordination Really be Counterproductive?' (processed).

Chrystal, K.A. (1987). 'Changing Perceptions of International Money and International Reserves in the World Economy,' in R.Z. Aliber, ed., *The Reconstruction of International Monetary Arrangements*, New York, St Martin's.

Collins, S.M. (1987). 'PPP and the Peso Problem' (processed).

—— (1988). 'Inflation and the EMS,' in F. Giavazzi, S. Micossi, and M. Miller, eds., *The European Monetary System*, Cambridge, Cambridge University Press.

Cooper, R.N. (1984). 'A Monetary System for the Future,' *Foreign Affairs*, 63, Fall.

—— (1985). 'Economic Interdependence and Coordination of Economic Policies,' in R.W. Jones and P.B. Kenen, eds., *Handbook of International Economics*, vol. 2, Amsterdam, North Holland.

Crockett, A., and M. Goldstein (1987). *Strengthening the International Monetary System: Exchange Rates, Surveillance, and Objective Indicators*, Washington, International Monetary Fund.

Currie, D., P. Levine, and N. Vidalis (1987). 'International Cooperation and Reputation in an Empirical Two-Block Model,' in R.C. Bryant and R. Portes, eds., *Global Macroeconomics: Policy Conflict and Cooperation*, London, Macmillan.

Currie, D., and S. Wren-Lewis (1988). 'A Comparison of Alternative Regimes for International Macropolicy Coordination' (processed).

Deputies of the Group of 10 (1985). *Report on the Functioning of the International Monetary System*, Washington, International Monetary Fund, *IMF Survey: Supplement*, July.

de Vries, M.G. (1987). *Balance of Payments Adjustment, 1945 to 1986: The IMF Experience*, Washington, International Monetary Fund.

Dixit, A. (1987). 'Entry and Exit Decisions of Firms under Fluctuating Real Exchange Rates' (processed).

Dominguez, K.M. (1986a). 'Are Foreign Exchange Forecasts Rational? New Evidence from Survey Data,' International Finance Discussion Paper 281, Washington, Board of Governors of the Federal Reserve System.

—— (1986b). 'Does Sterilized Intervention Influence Exchange Rates: A Test of the Signaling Hypothesis' (processed).

Dornbusch, R. (1976). 'Expectations and Exchange Rate Dynamics,' *Journal of Political Economy*, 84, August.

—— (1988). 'Doubts About the McKinnon Standard,' *Journal of Economic Perspectives*, 1, Winter.

Dornbusch, R., and J. Frankel (1987). 'The Flexible Exchange Rate System: Experience and Alternatives,' Working Paper 2464, Cambridge, National Bureau of Economic Research.

References

Driffill, J. (1988). 'The Stability and Sustainability of the EMS with Perfect Capital Markets,' in F. Giavazzi, S. Micossi, and M. Miller, eds., *The European Monetary System*, Cambridge, Cambridge University Press.

Eichengreen, B. (1985). 'International Policy Coordination in Historical Perspective,' in W.H. Buiter and R.C. Marston, eds., *International Economic Policy Coordination*, Cambridge, Cambridge University Press.

Feldstein, M. (1986). 'New Evidence on the Effects of Exchange Rate Intervention,' Working Paper 2052, Cambridge, National Bureau of Economic Research.

—— (1987). 'The End of Policy Coordination,' *The Wall Street Journal*, 9 November.

Fischer, S. (1988). 'Macroeconomic Policy,' in M. Feldstein, ed., *International Economic Cooperation*, Chicago, University of Chicago Press.

Flood, R.P., and P.M. Garber (1984). 'Collapsing Exchange Regimes: Some Linear Examples,' *Journal of International Economics*, 17, August.

Frankel, J.A. (1987a). 'Ambiguous Macroeconomic Policy Multipliers, in Theory and in Twelve Econometric Models,' Working Paper 8725, Berkeley, Department of Economics, University of California.

—— (1987b). 'Obstacles to International Macroeconomic Policy Coordination,' Working Paper 8737, Berkeley, Department of Economics, University of California.

Frankel, J.A., and K.A. Froot (1986). 'Explaining the Demand for Dollars: International Rates of Return and the Expectations of Chartists and Fundamentalists,' Working Paper 8603, Berkeley, Department of Economics, University of California.

Frankel, J.A., and K.A. Froot (1987). 'Using Survey Data to Test Standard Propositions Regarding Exchange Rate Expectations,' *American Economic Review*, 77, March.

Frankel, J.A., and K. Rockett (1988). 'International Macroeconomic Policy Coordination when Policy-Makers Do Not Agree on the True Model,' *American Economic Review*, 78, June.

Frankel, J.A. (1987). 'The International Monetary System: Should It Be Reformed?,' *American Economic Review*, 77, May.

Frankel, J.A., and M. Goldstein (1986). 'A Guide to Target Zones,' *IMF Staff Papers*, 33, December.

Funabashi, Y. (1988). *Managing the Dollar: From the Plaza to the Louvre*, Washington, Institute for International Economics.

Giavazzi, F., and A. Giovannini (1988). 'Models of the EMS: Is Europe a Greater Deutschemark Area?,' in R.C. Bryant and R. Portes, eds., *Global Macroeconomics: Policy Conflict and Cooperation*, London, Macmillan.

Giavazzi, F., and M. Pagano (1986). 'The Advantages of Tying One's Hands: EMS Discipline and Central Bank Credibility,' Discussion Paper 235, London, Centre for Economic Policy Research.

Grassman, S. (1976). 'Currency Distribution and Forward Cover in Foreign Trade,' *Journal of International Economics*, 6, May.

Grilli, V.U. (1986). 'Buying and Selling Attacks on Fixed Exchange Rate Systems,' *Journal of International Economics*, 20, February.

Gros, D., and N. Thygesen (1988). 'The EMS: Achievements, Current Issues and Directions for the Future' (processed).

Group of Thirty (1982). *How Central Banks Manage their Reserves*, New York.

Hamada, K. (1974). 'Alternative Exchange Rate Systems and the Interdependence of Monetary Policies,' in R.Z. Aliber, ed., *National Monetary Policies and the International Financial System*, Chicago, University of Chicago Press.

—— (1976). 'A Strategic Analysis of Monetary Interdependence,' *Journal of Political Economy*, 84, August.

Hodrick, R.J., and S. Srivastava (1984). 'An Investigation of Risk and Return in Forward Foreign Exchange,' *Journal of International Money and Finance*, 3, March.

Holtham, G., and A.J. Hughes Hallett (1987). 'International Policy Cooperation and Model Uncertainty' in R.C. Bryant and R. Portes, eds., *Global Macroeconomics: Policy Conflict and Cooperation*, Cambridge, Cambridge University Press.

Hsieh, D.A. (1984). 'Tests of Rational Expectations and No Risk Premium in Forward Exchange Markets,' *Journal of International Economics*, 17, August.

Hughes Hallett, A.J. (1987). 'Macroeconomic Policy Design with Incomplete Information: A New Argument for Coordinating Economic Policies,' Discussion Paper 151, London, Centre for Economic Policy Research.

International Monetary Fund (1974). *International Monetary Reform: Documents of the Committee of Twenty*, Washington.

Kenen, P.B. (1969). 'The Theory of Optimum Currency Areas: An Eclectic View,' in *Essays in International Economics*, Princeton, Princeton University Press, 1980.

—— (1973). 'Convertibility and Consolidation: Options for Reform of the International Monetary System,' in *Essays in International Economics*, Princeton, Princeton University Press, 1980.

—— (1975). 'Floats, Glides, and Indicators: A Comparison of Methods for Changing Exchange Rates,' in *Essays in International Economics*, Princeton, Princeton University Press, 1980.

—— (1976). *Capital Mobility and Financial Integration: A Survey*, Princeton Studies in International Finance 39, Princeton, International Finance Section, Princeton University.

References

Kenen, P.B. (1981). 'The Analytics of a Substitution Account,' *Banca Nazionale Del Lavoro Quarterly Review*, December.

—— (1983a). *The Role of the Dollar as an International Currency*, New York, Group of Thirty.

—— (1983b). 'Use of the SDR to Supplement or Substitute for Other Means of Finance,' in G.M. von Furstenberg, ed., *International Money and Credit: The Policy Roles*, Washington, International Monetary Fund.

—— (1986). *Financing, Adjustment, and the International Monetary Fund*, Washington, The Brookings Institution.

—— (1987a). 'Exchange Rates and Policy Coordination,' Discussion Paper in International Economics 61, Washington, The Brookings Institution.

—— (1987b). 'What Role for IMF Surveillance?,' *World Development*, 15.

—— (1988). 'International Money and Macroeconomics,' in K.A. Elliott and J. Williamson, eds., *World Economic Problems*, Washington, Institute for International Economics.

Keynes, J.M. (1936). *The General Theory of Employment, Interest and Money*, London, Macmillan.

Kindleberger, C.P. (1986). 'International Public Goods without International Government,' *American Economic Review*, 76, March.

Krugman, P.R. (1979). 'A Model of Balance-of-Payments Crises,' *Journal of Money, Credit and Banking*, 11, August.

—— (1980). 'Vehicle Currencies and the Structure of International Exchange,' *Journal of Money, Credit and Banking*, 13, August.

—— (1987). 'The Bias in the Band: Exchange Rate Expectations under a Broad-Band Exchange Rate Regime' (processed).

—— (1988a). 'An Imperfectly Integrated World: The Robbins Memorial Lectures' (processed).

—— (1988b). 'Louvre's Lesson – Let the Dollar Fall,' *The International Economy*, January/February.

—— (1988c). 'Target Zones and Exchange Rate Dynamics,' Working Paper 2481, Cambridge, National Bureau of Economic Research.

Krugman, P.R., and R.E. Baldwin (1987). 'The Persistence of the US Trade Deficit,' *Brookings Papers on Economic Activity*, 1.

League of Nations (1944). *International Currency Experience*.

Levich, R.M. (1985). 'Empirical Studies of Exchange Rates: Price Behavior, Rate Determination and Market Efficiency,' in R.W.Jones and P.B. Kenen, eds., *Handbook of International Economics*, vol. 2, Amsterdam, North Holland.

Lewis, K.K. (1986). 'Testing for the Effectiveness of Sterilized Foreign Exchange Market Intervention Using a Structural Multilateral Asset Market Approach,' Working Paper 372, New York, Salomon Brothers Centre for the Study of Financial Institutions, New York University.

Loopesko, B.E. (1983). 'Relationships among Exchange Rates, Intervention, and Interest Rates: An Empirical Investigation,' Staff Studies 133, Washington, Board of Governors of the Federal Reserve Board.

McKibbin, W.J., and J.D. Sachs (1986). 'Comparing the Global Performance of Alternative Exchange Rate Arrangements,' Discussion Paper in International Economics 49, Washington, The Brookings Institution.

McKinnon, R.I. (1984). *An International Standard for Monetary Stabilization*, Policy Analyses in International Economics 8, Washington, Institute for International Economics.

—— (1988). 'Monetary and Exchange Rate Policies for International Financial Stability,' *Journal of Economic Perspectives*, 1, Winter.

Marris, S. (1987). *Deficits and the Dollar: The World Economy at Risk*, Policy Analyses in International Economics 14 (rev. edn), Washington, Institute for International Economics.

Masera, R.S. (1987). 'European Currency: An Italian View' (processed).

Mastropasqua, C., S. Micossi, and R. Rinaldi (1988). 'Intervention, Sterilization and Monetary Policy in EMS Countries, 1979–1987,' in F. Giavazzi, S. Micossi, and M. Miller, eds., *The European Monetary System*, Cambridge, Cambridge University Press.

Meade, J.E. (1984). 'A New Keynesian Bretton Woods,' *Three Banks Review*, June.

Meese, R.A., and K. Rogoff (1983). 'Empirical Exchange Rates Models of the Seventies: Do They Fit Out of Sample?,' *Journal of International Economics*, 14, February.

Melitz, J. (1987). 'Monetary Discipline and Cooperation in the EMS: A Synthesis,' Discussion Paper 219, London, Centre for Economic Policy Research.

Melitz, J., and P. Michel (1988). 'The Dynamic Stability of the European Monetary System' (processed).

Micossi, S. (1985). 'The Intervention and Financing Mechanisms of the EMS and the Role of the ECU,' *Banca Nazionale del Lavoro Quarterly Review*, December.

Mundell, R.A. (1962). 'The Appropriate Use of Monetary and Fiscal Policy under Fixed Exchange Rates,' *IMF Staff Papers*, March.

—— (1969). 'Problems of the International Monetary System,' in R.A. Mundell and A.K. Swoboda, eds., *Monetary Problems of the International Economy*, Chicago, University of Chicago Press.

Obstfeld, M. (1983). 'Exchange Rates, Inflation, and the Sterilization Problem: Germany, 1975–1981,' *European Economic Review*, 21, March.

—— (1984). 'Balance-of-Payments Crises and Devaluation,' *Journal of Money, Credit and Banking*, 16, May.

References

Obstfeld, M. (1986). 'Rational and Self-Fulfilling Balance-of-Payments Crises,' *American Economic Review*, 76, March.

—— (1988). 'Competitiveness, Realignment and Speculation: The Role of Financial Markets,' in F. Giavazzi, S. Micossi, and M. Miller, eds., *The European Monetary System*, Cambridge, Cambridge University Press.

Oudiz, G., and J. Sachs (1984). 'Macroeconomic Policy Coordination Among the Industrial Economies,' *Brookings Papers on Economic Activity*, 1.

Oudiz, G., and J. Sachs (1985). 'International Policy Coordination in Dynamic Macroeconomic Models,' in W.H. Buiter and R.C. Marston, eds., *International Economic Policy Coordination*, Cambridge, Cambridge University Press.

Persson, T. (1987). 'Credibility of Macroeconomic Policy: An Introduction and a Broad Survey,' Seminar Paper 193, Stockholm, Institute for International Economic Studies.

Putnam, R.D., and N. Bayne (1987). *Hanging Together: The Seven-Power Summits* (2nd edn), London, Sage Publications.

Putnam, R.D., and C.R. Henning (1986). 'The Bonn Summit of 1978: How Does International Economic Policy Coordination Really Work?,' Discussion Paper in International Economics 53, Washington, The Brookings Institution.

Rogoff, K. (1984). 'On the Effects of Sterilized Intervention: An Analysis of Weekly Data,' *Journal of Monetary Economics*, 13, September.

—— (1985). 'Can International Monetary Cooperation be Counterproductive?,' *Journal of International Economics*, 18, May.

Solomon, R. (1982). *The International Monetary System, 1945-1981*, New York, Harper & Row.

Triffin, R. (1960). *Gold and the Dollar Crisis*, New Haven, Yale University Press.

Tsoukalis, L. (1987). 'The Political Economy of the European Monetary System' (processed).

Ungerer, H., O. Evans, T. Mayer, and P. Young (1986). *The European Monetary System: Recent Developments*, Washington, International Monetary Fund.

Williamson, J. (1977). *The Failure of World Monetary Reform*, New York, NYU Press.

—— (1982). 'The Failure of World Monetary Reform: A Reassessment,' in R.N. Cooper, et al., eds., *The International Monetary System under Flexible Exchange Rates*, Cambridge, Ballinger.

—— (1985). *The Exchange Rate System*, Policy Analyses in International Economics 5 (2nd edn), Washington, Institute for International Economics.

Williamson, J., and M.H. Miller (1987). *Targets and Indicators; A Blueprint for the International Coordination of Economic Policies*,

Policy Analyses in International Economics 22, Washington, Institute for International Economics.

Working Group on Exchange Market Intervention (1983). *Report*, Washington, US Treasury.